Learning
Excel 2013
with 100 Practical Exercises

Learning
Excel 2013
with 100 Practical Exercises

MCB
Press
www.mcb-press.com

Learning Excel 2013 with 100 Practical Exercises

Copyright © 2014 MEDIAactive

First edition: July 2014

Published by © MCB Press, distributed in USA and Canada by ATLAS BOOKS, 30 Amberwood Parkway, Ashland, Ohio 44805. To contact a representative, please e-mail us at order@bookmasters.com.

Distributed in Europe by MCB Press. To contact a representative, please contact us at info@mcb-press.com, Facebook or Twitter.

www.mcb-press.com

Cover Designer: NDENU DISSENY GRÀFIC

ISBN: 978-84-267-2011-5

Printed in EU

Presentation

LEARNING EXCEL 2013 WITH 100 PRACTICAL EXERCISES

These 100 practical exercises provide a tour of the main functions of the program. While it is impossible to include all the features of Excel 2013 in the pages of this book, we have chosen the most interesting and useful ones. Once you have completed the 100 exercises that make up this book, you will be able to use the program with ease the program and create and edit different types of workbooks, both personally and professionally.

THE LEARNING METHOD

Our experience in the field of education has led us to design this type of manual, where you complete each of the program's functions by performing a practical exercise. These exercises are explained step-by-step and click by click, so that they are easy to follow and complete. Furthermore, each exercise is illustrated with descriptive images of the most important steps or the results to be obtained, and IMPORTANT boxes provide further information about each of the topics covered in the exercises.

This system ensures that after completing the 100 exercises that make up this book, the user can confidently use Excel 2013 tools and take advantage of the many benefits offered by the program.

THE NECESSARY FILES

In case you want to use the sample files mentioned in this book, you can download them from the download section of the Marcombo website (www.marcombo.com) and from the specific page of this book.

WHO SHOULD READ THIS BOOK

If you are a beginner using and working with Excel 2013, you will find a complete tour of its main functions in these pages. However, if you are an expert at using this program, you will also find this book useful to learn about the improvements in this version or to review specific functions you can find in the index.

Each exercise is treated independently, so it isn't necessary to complete them in order (even though we recommend it, as we have attempted to group exercises around common topics). Thus, if you need to find out about something in particular, you can go directly to the specific exercise on the subject and complete it on your own Excel document.

EXCEL 2013

Microsoft Excel is one of the more powerful spreadsheet programs in the computing market and at the same time it is very easy to use. This second feature should be stressed, since a program capable of performing the most complicated calculations would be useless to the public if its learning process were long and hard.

A spreadsheet is designed to make all kinds of numerical calculations automatically, following the guidelines set by the user.

With Microsoft Excel you can build many types of spreadsheets and even databases like diaries or phone lists that can store the names of clients, or contact phone numbers, etc. The interface of the new Excel 2013, in addition to having a nice design, is improved in this new version. It features a large number of wizards that facilitate the task of representing the user's data in PivotTables or professional looking graphics.

How *Learning...* books work

The title of each exercise undoubtedly expresses what it consists of. Thus, if you are interested, you can go directly to the exercise you want to learn or review.

The exercises are written systematically step-by-step, so you don't ever miss anything during the implementation of the exercise.

The number on the right-hand side of the page tells you clearly what exercise you are on.

IMPORTANT boxes include actions that must be done to ensure you complete each exercise properly. They also contain tips that will facilitate your work with the program.

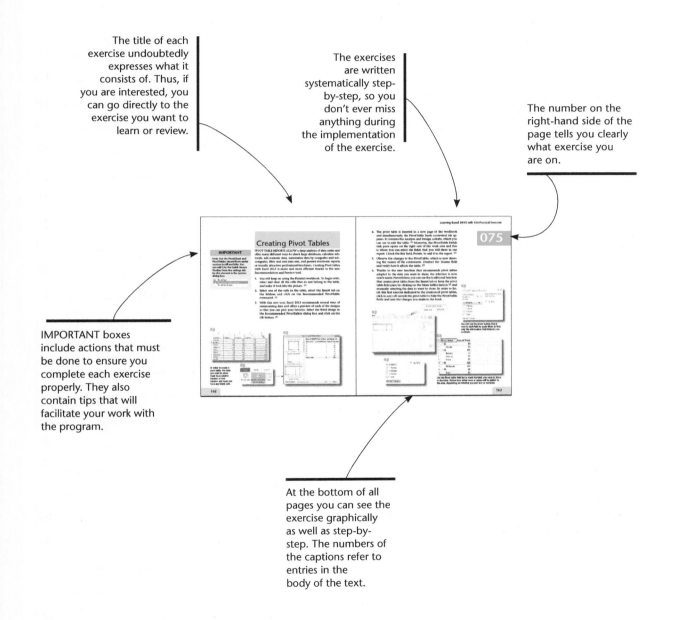

At the bottom of all pages you can see the exercise graphically as well as step-by-step. The numbers of the captions refer to entries in the body of the text.

Table of contents

Table of contents

The new Excel 2013: Quick Start

EXCEL IS ONE OF THE MOST WIDELY USED, best known, and most common spreadsheet office IT application. It allows you to organize large amounts of data, track different kinds of information, and carry out mathematical operations ranging from the simplest sums, subtraction and division, to the most complex trigonometric functions. In this first exercise, you will open Excel and make your first contact with the application's Quick Start window.

1. Move through the Windows 8 **Start** screen until you locate the Excel 2013 application tile, and click on it. 🔲 (If you are working with an earlier version of the operating system, you can open Excel from the **All Programs** option in the traditional **Start** menu).

2. If you have worked with earlier versions of the program, you will notice the newer, cleaner look, designed to help you obtain professional results with minimum effort. When opening Excel 2013, you will see the Quick Start window, 🔲 from which you can quickly access the workbooks you have worked with recently (which will be added to the **Recent** panel on the left), open other workbooks or create a new blank workbook or workbook based on the numerous templates offered by the program. Click on the lower part of the **verticle scroll bar** on the list of screens to see some of the available options.

In Windows 8, tiles for the apps installed on your computer are added to the **Start** screen. If you do not have this tile, you can look for it using the operating system's new **Search** function.

3. As you can see, Excel 2013 offers a large number of different templates in different categories to make your job easier when you need to create your own templates. Click, for instance, on the **Invoice** category in the **Suggested searches** section. 🗩**3**

4. The program automatically runs an online search and displays the templates that correspond to this category in the **New** window. Notice that all existing categories, along with the number of templates provided by Excel, are listed in the **Category** panel. You can also carry out custom searches by entering a keyword in the search field. Enter the word **Orders** in that field, for instance, and click on the magnifying glass icon to continue with the search. 🗩**4**

5. See what some of these templates look like. Click on the second result, **Work order tracker**. 🗩**5**

6. This opens a preview window in which you can see the main properties of the template and from which you can create your own file based on it. Click on the **Create** button. 🗩**6**

7. Once the template is open, you can modify it according to your own needs and save the file under a new name. To close the template, click on the **File** tab and choose the **Close** option in the menu that appears.

8. Specify that you do not want to save your changes to the template by clicking on the **Don't Save** button in the warning screen.

IMPORTANT

You can also create new documents directly based on templates without going through the preview by using the **Create** option in their pop-up menus.

5

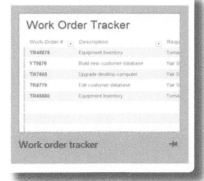

3

Search for online templates

Suggested searches: Budget Invoice Calendars Expense

Templates allow you to concentrate on figures rather than design and document configuration.

4

New

🏠 Home   Orders   🔎

The Preview window for templates allows you to see their **download size** and their **user rating**.

6

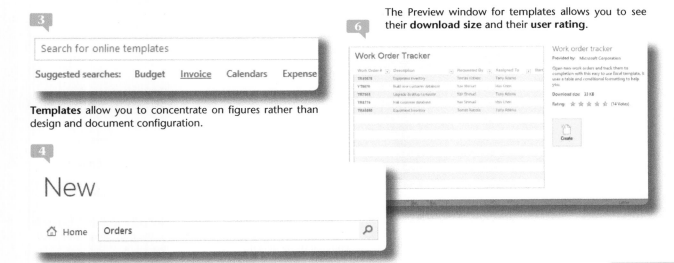

The Quick Access Toolbar

THE QUICK ACCESS TOOLBAR is located to the left of the Title Bar. It contains icons for the three most common actions that are carried out with documents: Save, Undo, and Redo. This is a customizable bar to which you can add new icons from the customization category in the Excel Options window or by using the appropriate option in the tools' pop-up menus.

1. In this exercise you will learn how to add icons to the **Quick Access Toolbar** in two different ways. Click on the arrow button on this bar and click on the **More Commands** option.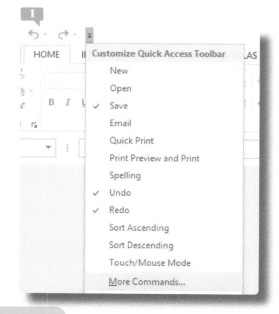

2. This opens the **Excel Options** window, displaying the **Quick Access Toolbar** category that is active. Here, different categories that contain the tools are listed. Select, for instance, the **Open** tool and click on the **Add** button.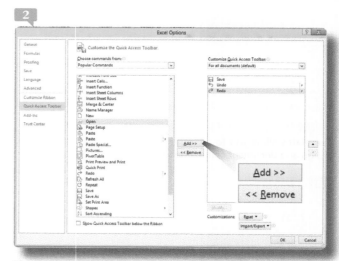

3. The **Open** tool icon should appear on the bar. Notice that any changes you make to the bar can either affect all documents you open with Excel, or only the currently open one. You can remove unwanted icons by selecting them in the box on the right and clicking on the **Remove** button. Likewise, the arrows to the right of the icon box allow you to set the

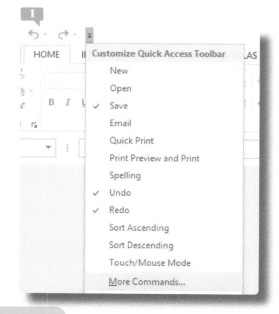

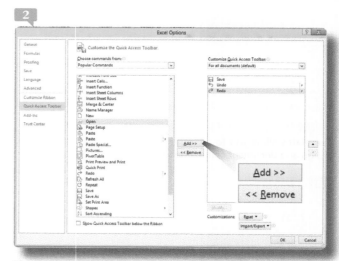

The **Popular Commands** menu contains the most frequently used commands by default.

order in which they are displayed on the bar. Click on the **Reset** button.

4. Two reset options will be displayed **3** and selecting the first one will open the **Reset Customizations** window. Click on the **Yes** button **4** to return the Quick Access Toolbar to its original look and close the **Excel Options** window by clicking on the **Cancel** button.

5. There is a somewhat quicker way to add icons to this bar. Assume you want the Cell tool group. In the **Home** tab on the **Ribbon**, right-click on the title of the **Cells** tool group, and click on the **Add to Quick Access Toolbar** option from its pop-up menu. **5**

6. As you can see, you can not only add icons but tool groups as well. Click on the **Cells** icon you added to the **Quick Access Toolbar** **6** and, after noticing that it includes several tools to work with cells, click on it again to hide them.

7. To delete this tool group from the **Quick Access Toolbar**, right-click on it and choose the **Remove from Quick Access Toolbar** option.

002

IMPORTANT

The **Touch/Mouse Mode** tool is a new feature in Excel 2013 that allows you to change from the usual mouse mode to touch mode, which is useful for mobile devices as it expands the buttons in the Ribbon to make it easier to use on touch screens.

Touch/Mouse Mode

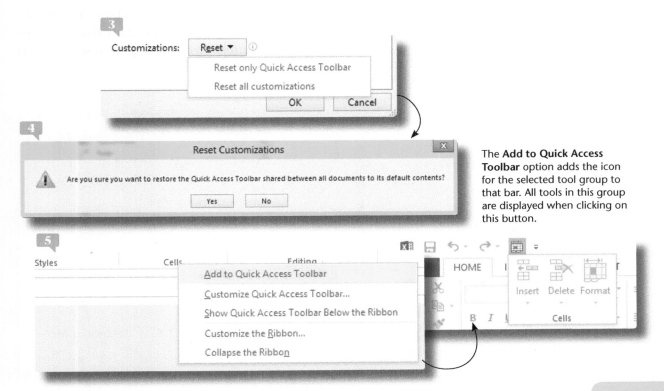

The **Add to Quick Access Toolbar** option adds the icon for the selected tool group to that bar. All tools in this group are displayed when clicking on this button.

Practice using the Ribbon

THE RIBBON was designed to assist you in the task of finding the necessary commands to carry out actions. Each tab in the ribbon contains groups related to a specific activity (insert, page design, enter formulas, etc.). To move from one tab to another, simply click on it.

1. Begin this exercise with a new blank workbook open in Excel. By default, the **Home** tab is active tab when starting the application. In order to view the contents of the **Page Layout** tab, click on it. **1**

2. Notice that there is a small icon next to the title of some tool groups. This is the dialog box or options panel starter. Click on this icon in the **Page Setup** group, for instance. **2**

3. In this case, you have opened the **Page Setup** window, from which you can set the properties that will apply to your page for printing. Close it by clicking on the **Cancel** button. **3**

4. Apart from the eight tabs that appear by default in the **Ribbon**, there are a series of contextual tool tabs that only appear when an item to which their tools apply is selected, to

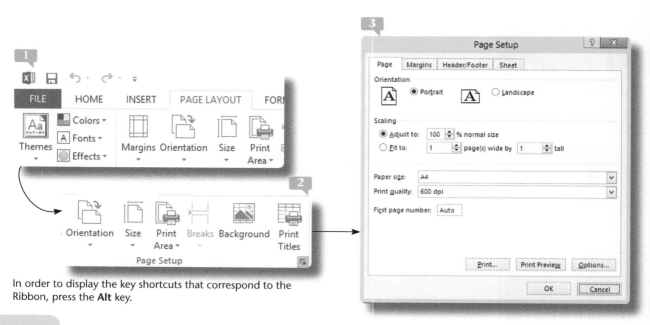

In order to display the key shortcuts that correspond to the Ribbon, press the **Alt** key.

avoid unnecessary confusion. Click on the **Insert** tab and click on the **Table** tool, in the **Tables** tool group. 4️⃣

5. Keep the settings that appear in the **Create Table** window and click on the **OK** button. 5️⃣

6. A table is automatically created in the selected cell, and a new tab, called **Table Tools**, appears in the **Ribbon**, along with a new subtab called **Design**. Click on the **More** button in the **Table Styles** group. 6️⃣

7. This opens an extensive gallery of table styles 7️⃣ that allows you to modify the look of your table. Move the cursor over the style you prefer and notice how the program displays a preview on the table you created before applying the style. 8️⃣ In order to apply the style permanently, click on it.

8. Click on the **A1** cell and, while keeping the **Shift** key pressed down, click on the **A2** cell and press the **Delete** key to delete the table from your spreadsheet.

003

IMPORTANT

Another new feature in Excel 2013 is the ability to hide the Ribbon automatically and to display it only when you need to by clicking on the upper part of the application. To do so, use the appropriate option in the **Ribbon Display Options** menu.

The live preview allows you to see what an item will look like when you apply a style to it before choosing it permanently.

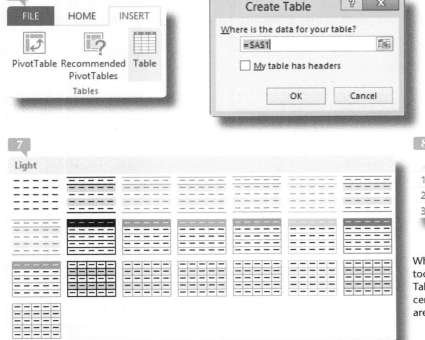

When inserting a table in a spreadsheet, a tool tab for this item appears in the Ribbon. Tabs of this type are only displayed when certain objects are selected or certain views are enabled.

Customizing the Excel environment

IN THE EXCEL OPTIONS DIALOG BOX, which you can open from the improved File menu, there are several commands that allow you to change the program environment. Some of these options are also available in the Account option in this same menu.

1. Click on the **File** tab and click on the **Options** command.

2. You can choose whether or not to display the **Mini Toolbar**, whose tools allow you to modify the contents of cells, when you select it, to enable or disable active previews, display the new quick analysis options, etc., in the **General** tab. Take a look at the backgrounds offered by the program. Click on the arrow button in the **Office Background** field, in the **Personalize your copy of Microsoft Office** section, and choose the **Stars** option.

3. In the **When creating new** work**books** section, you can set the font and text size to be used by default as well as set the default view for sheets and the number of sheets to be included in new workbooks, which is 1 by default in this version of the program. Click on the **Advanced** category in the panel on the left.

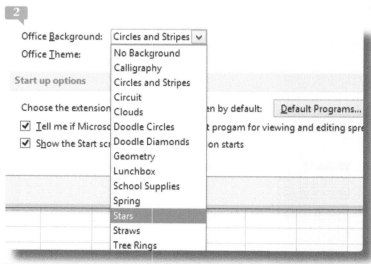

The **Personalize your copy of Microsoft Office** section also allows you to modify the user name and the default Office theme.

004

4. This tab contains other settings for the Excel environment. Change the number of recent workbooks to be displayed by the program in the Quick Start window. Scroll down with the vertical scroll bar, double-click on the **Show this number of Recent Workbooks** field and type in a different value.

5. You can also display or hide the **Formula Bar**, the scroll bars, and the row and column headings. Disable the **Show formula bar** option in the **Display** field. ▸**3**

6. Continue moving down, disable the **Show row and column headers** option in the **Display options for this worksheet** section ▸**4** and click on the **OK** button to apply the changes.

7. The change in the application background is apparent, as is the removal of the row and column headings and the **Formula Bar**. Go to the **View** tab in the **Ribbon** by clicking on its tab.

8. From here you can change the workbook views, display or hide items, change the zoom level, and organize windows when there is more than one open. Enable the **Formula Bar** and **Headings** options in the **Show** group. ▸**5**

9. In order to return to the original background, go to the **Account** option in the **File** tab and choose the **Circles and Stripes** option in the **Office Background** command. ▸**6**

IMPORTANT

The **Advanced** category in the Excel Options window also allows you quick access to recent workbooks and to change the number of recent unpinned folders. Furthermore, the **General** category also allows you to disable the Start window when opening the application.

The **Show** tool group in the View tab allows you to display or hide the Ruler, Gridlines, Formula Bar, and Headings.

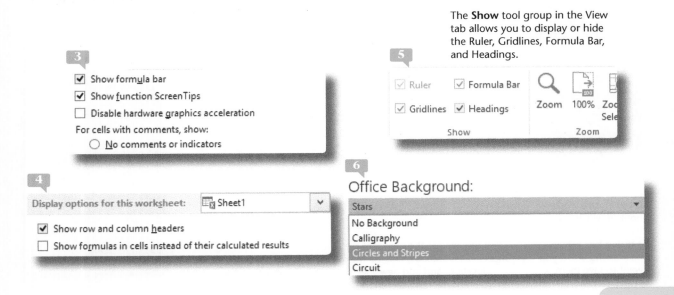

3
- ✔ Show form**u**la bar
- ✔ Show **f**unction ScreenTips
- ☐ Disable hardware **g**raphics acceleration

For cells with comments, show:
- ◯ **N**o comments or indicators

4

Display options for this work**s**heet: ▣ Sheet1 ▾
- ✔ Show row and column **h**eaders
- ☐ Show fo**r**mulas in cells instead of their calculated results

5
- ☑ Ruler   ☑ Formula Bar   🔍 Zoom   100%   Zoo...
- ☑ Gridlines ☑ Headings   Sele...

Show   Zoom

6
Office Background:
Stars ▾
No Background
Calligraphy
Circles and Stripes
Circuit

Opening spreadsheets and workbooks

DOCUMENTS CREATED WITH EXCEL are called workbooks. Each one of them is made up of several spreadsheets saved in the same file. A spreadsheet is a rectangular grid made up of a certain number of cells organized in rows and columns.

1. The **Title Bar** displays the default name given to Excel documents. Click on the **File** tab and close the workbook by clicking on the **Close** option.

2. If you have made changes to the workbook, the program will ask you if you want to save it on your computer. Click on the **Don't Save** button in the dialog box.

3. Click on the **File** tab again. Select the **New** option to create a blank workbook and click on the **Blank workbook** option.

4. Notice the title of the new workbook which, like the first one, is made up of one sheet. Repeat the previous step to create a second blank workbook.

5. As a new feature in Excel 2013, each workbook has its own window, to make working with two workbooks easier if you are, for instance, working with two monitors. Click on the **Minimize size** button in the **Title Bar** of the last book you have opened and notice how the two windows of the two open books are displayed.

	A	B	C
1			
2			
3			
4			
5			
6			
7			

Blank workbook

If you close a workbook in which you have made changes, a dialog box will appear asking you if you want to save them.

You can change the names of the sheets in a workbook, change their location, and add new sheets.

6. Edit the tab of the workbook that is displayed in front. Double click on the **Sheet1** tab to display it in edit mode, assign a new name to the sheet, and press the **Enter** key.

7. To open a book saved on your computer, click on the **File** tab and click on the **Open** command.

8. If you do not have any Excel files saved on your computer, you can download the **Points.xlsx** document from our website and save it on your computer. Click on the **Computer** option in the new **Open** window.

9. Excel 2013 allows you to open your recent folders to find the file you wish to open or to search in all folders with the **Browse** button. Click on this button, look for and select your file in the **Open** window, and click on the **Open** button.

10. Select a cell with contents and notice that they are also displayed in the **Formula Bar**, whether they are text or numbers.

11. If it is the result of a formula, as in the illustration, the formula will be displayed in the bar. In order to delete the contents of the selected cell, press the **Delete** key.

12. If this cell is a part of a formula, you will see how it is updated automatically. Having learned how a spreadsheet works at a basic level, save your changes, if you want to, by clicking on the **Save** icon, represented by a diskette in the **Quick Access Toolbar.**

IMPORTANT

You can also change the name of the sheet by using the **Rename** option in its tab's pop-up menu.

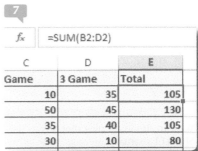

C	D	E
Game	3 Game	Total
10	35	105
50	45	130
35	40	105
30	10	80

f_x =SUM(B2:D2)

When changing the components in a formula, the final results are updated automatically and displayed in the appropriate cell.

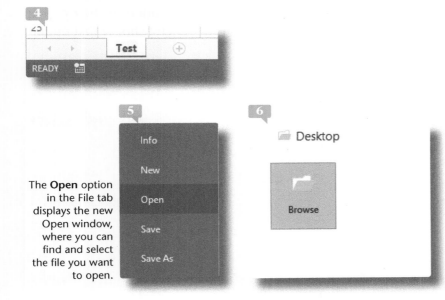

The **Open** option in the File tab displays the new Open window, where you can find and select the file you want to open.

Inserting sheets and navigating through them

IMPORTANT

If you want to insert several worksheets at a time, press and hold the **Shift** key, and then select the same number of existing sheets you want to insert in the open workbook.

YOU CAN USE THE INSERT BUTTON on the Home tab to insert new sheets, the New sheet icon that appears to the right of the sheet tabs, or the Insert option in sheets' pop-up menus. There are also many ways to move through worksheets by using the mouse, keyboard, or shortcuts.

1. An Excel 2013 workbook has one sheet by default. Remember that you can change this start-up setting in the **Excel Options** window. Begin with a blank workbook open in the program. To insert a sheet, click on the arrow button in the **Insert** tool, in the **Cells** group on the **Home** tab, and choose the **Insert Sheet** option.

2. By using this new method, the sheet is located to the left of the one that was previously selected, and it is named **Sheet2**, following numerical order. Here's another way to insert a sheet and move it. Right-click on the **Sheet2** tab and choose the **Insert** option.

3. You can see some of the objects that can be inserted in an Excel book in the **Insert** dialog box. Select the **Worksheet** option and click on the **OK** button.

4. To change the order of these sheets, you can drag them with the mouse or use the **Move or Copy** option in their pop-up menus. Right-click on the **Sheet3** tab and choose that option.

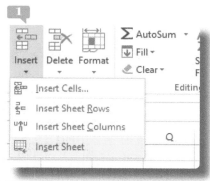

You can also insert new sheets with the **Shift+F1** shortcut.

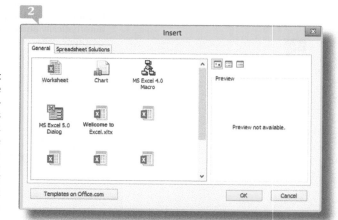

The **Insert** command in the sheet tab's pop-up menu opens the dialog box with the same name, in which you can choose which kind of items you want to insert.

5. In the options list in the **Move or Copy** window, select move to end and click on the **OK** button. 3️⃣

6. Insert a new sheet at the end of the workbook by using the **Insert Worksheet** icon, to the right of the sheet tabs. 4️⃣

7. To move through the cells in a sheet, simply select them with your mouse. For instance, click on the **D9** cell in the sheet you just inserted. 5️⃣

8. You can also move through cells using your keyboard. Click on the up arrow key to move to the **D8** cell, and then click on the **Next page** key to move one entire screen down.

9. Press **Ctrl+right arrow** to move to the end of the row. 6️⃣

10. Keep in mind that if there was a cell with contents within the active row, the cursor would have stopped in it. Press the **Home** key.

11. The move has taken you to the first cell in the row. There is a direct way of accessing a cell that is not visible on-screen. Click on the **Find & Select** tool in the **Editing** tool group, and select **Go To** from the options list. 7️⃣

12. In the **Reference** field of the **Go To** dialog box, type **K9**, for instance, and click on the **OK** button.

13. You can use the **Go To** window to access any specific cell in a sheet directly: first, insert the name of the sheet, and, after an exclamation point, the cell name (for example: **Sheet1!A3**). Click on the **Sheet2** tab to go to this sheet and save your workbook.

IMPORTANT

Excel 2013 has 1,048,576 rows and 16,384 columns.

The **Ctrl+right arrow** shortcut moves you to the last cell in the row wherein the selected cell is.

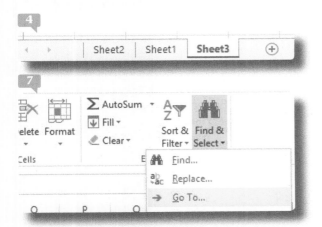

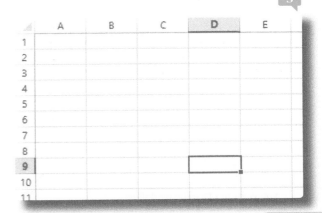

Moving sheets and freezing panes

AS YOU SAW IN THE PREVIOUS EXERCISE, you can move sheets and change their order by dragging a worksheet's tab to the point where you want to place it or by using the options in their pop-up menus. The Freeze Panes, Freeze Top Row, and Freeze First Column functions, included in the Freeze Panes command on the View tab, allow you to keep these items still so that they remain visible when moving through the worksheet.

1. Let's assume you want to put **Sheet1** first in the Sheet Tab Bar. Click on the **Sheet1** tab and drag it over the **Sheet2** tab. 🗨

2. The **Sheet1** tab is now to the right of **Sheet2** and it remains active. Place **Sheet3** in front of **Sheet2**. Right-click on the **Sheet3** tab.

3. The sheet's pop-up menu appears. Click on the **Move or Copy** function. 🗨

4. This opens the **Move or Copy** window, which you can also open from the **Format** command in the **Cells** tool group, on the **Home** tab. The **To book** section allows you to select to which currently active workbook you want to move or copy

One way of moving sheets within a book is to directly drag their tabs to the place where you want to put them.

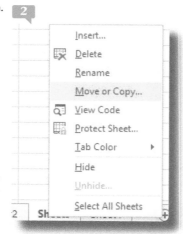

You can also open the **Move or Copy** window to specify the place in the workbook where you want to place the worksheet.

the currently selected sheet. You also must specify before which sheet you want to place the selected sheet in the **Before sheet** section. Select the **Sheet2** option in this box and click **OK**. 🔳

5. Now that you know both methods for moving sheets, return them to their logical positions by dragging them. Learn how to freeze parts of a sheet so that they remain visible when you move around the worksheet. Click on the **View** tab in the **Ribbon**.

6. Assume the first row in this sheet will contain the table's titles and you want to keep them visible all the time. Click on the **Freeze Panes** command in the **Window** tool group and click on the **Freeze Top** Row option. 🔳

7. A line appears beneath the top row, indicating that it is frozen. 🔳 Click on the lower part of the vertical scroll bar to check. 🔳

8. Also freeze the first column. Click on the **Freeze Panes** command again and click on the **Freeze First Column** option.

9. The top row is no longer frozen, and the first column will remain visible even if you move to the right. Try it by using the horizontal scroll bar.

10. Click on the **Freeze Panes** command again and choose the **Unfreeze Panes** option to return them to their original state.

007

IMPORTANT

To freeze rows and columns, select the cell below and to the right of the point where you want the division to appear and use the **Freeze Panes** option.

Notice that, when the top row is frozen, it does not move when you move the other rows. Even if you moved down to row 30, the first one will always be at the top. The same happens when you freeze a column.

Deleting sheets

YOU CAN REMOVE A SHEET FROM A BOOK using the Delete button in the Home tab on the Ribbon or by using the Delete option in the sheet tabs' pop-up menus.

1. Notice that when you try to delete a sheet with contents, Excel will prompt you with a warning message. Type any combination of numbers in the currently selected cell and press the **Enter** key to confirm it.

2. Click on the arrow button on the **Delete** tool, in the **Cells** group on the **Home** tab, and click on the **Delete Sheet** option.

3. This opens the Microsoft Excel window, in which the program tells you that the sheet contains information that will be permanently deleted if you carry out the operation. Click on the **Cancel** button in this dialog box so you do not delete the sheet.

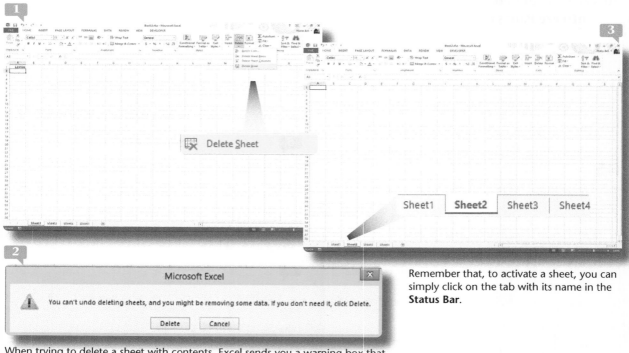

Delete Sheet

Sheet1   **Sheet2**   Sheet3   Sheet4

Remember that, to activate a sheet, you can simply click on the tab with its name in the **Status Bar**.

Microsoft Excel

You can't undo deleting sheets, and you might be removing some data. If you don't need it, click Delete.

Delete   Cancel

When trying to delete a sheet with contents, Excel sends you a warning box that allows you to cancel the action if you do not want to delete it permanently.

4. On the contrary, if the sheet is empty, the program deletes it directly, as you will see. Click on the tab of an empty sheet in your book.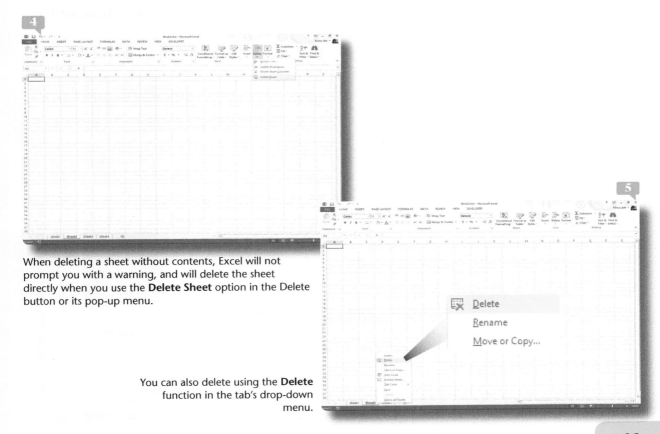

5. Click on the **Delete** tool's arrow button, in the **Cells** group, again, and select the **Delete Sheet** option.

6. The selected sheet is automatically deleted and the other sheets in the workbook move to the left, taking up the space left by the deleted sheet (unless it was the last sheet, in which case the positions of the other sheets will not change). You can also delete sheets by using the appropriate option in the pop-up menu of their tabs. Right-click on the tab of one of your sheets and, in the pop-up menu that appears, select the **Delete** option.

7. If the sheet you are trying to delete has contents in it, make sure they aren't important, as the information will be lost, and click on the **Delete** button in the dialog box.

008

IMPORTANT

Keep in mind that deleting sheets cannot be undone, so make sure the contents of the sheet are not important before deleting it as its contents will be lost forever.

When deleting a sheet without contents, Excel will not prompt you with a warning, and will delete the sheet directly when you use the **Delete Sheet** option in the Delete button or its pop-up menu.

You can also delete using the **Delete** function in the tab's drop-down menu.

Seeing file properties

IMPORTANT

The information contained in the **General** tab of the Properties window refers to the file size, creation or modification date, the number of words or characters in a document, etc.; these automatically updated properties cannot be specified or modified.

Type:	Microsoft Excel Worksheet
Location:	C:\Users\Nuria\Documents\Excel .
Size:	8.97KB (9,189 bytes)

MS-DOS name:	BOOK3~1.XLS
Created:	Monday, July 29, 2013 9:11

THE DOCUMENT PROPERTIES PANEL allows you to add data to workbooks to help you identify them, such as their author, title, subject, etc. Some of this information can be modified by the user, whereas some of it cannot be edited as they are a reflection of the actions carried out on the file.

1. Click on the **File** tab and enable the **Info** category.

2. In the so-called Backstage view, on the right of the options of the selected category, you can see some of the workbook's properties. Click on the **Properties** command and click on the **Show Document Panel** option.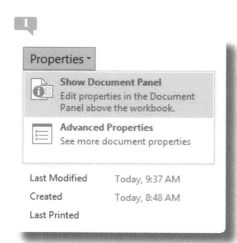

3. The **Document Properties** panel will appear over the tabs, displaying basic information about the workbook, from which you can access advanced properties. Click on the **Document Properties** command and select the **Advanced Properties** option.

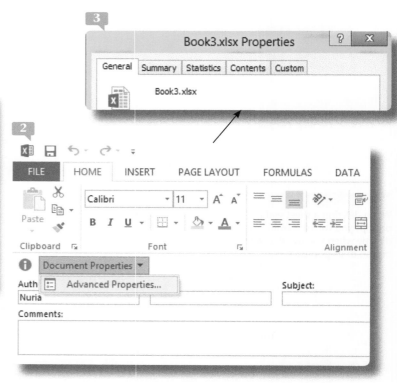

You can also access the Advanced Properties window from the Properties command in the **Info** category.

30

009

4. This opens the **Book** (book name) **Properties** window, displaying the **General** tab ▣ in which the file's general attributes are displayed. Click on the **Summary** tab.

5. You can enter information in this tab. For instance, in the **Title** text box, type in the word **Payment**. ▤

6. Locate the cursor in the **Manager** field and type in your name. ▥

7. Enter **Accounting** in the **Category** field.

8. The **Keywords** field is often used to enter words with which you can search for the file later on. Type **payment**, for instance, in this field. ▦

9. Click on the **Statistics** tab to check the type of information being saved, and do so with the **Contents** and **Custom** tabs as well.

10. The **Custom** tab allows you to include new properties for the document. Select the **Department** option in the **Name** field, click on the **Value** field, and type **Accountant**.

11. Click on the **Add** ▧ button to confirm the action and exit the Advanced Properties panel by clicking on the **OK** button.

Notice that the **Document Properties** panel has been updated with the new file information you added. To close this panel, use the **X** button on its right.

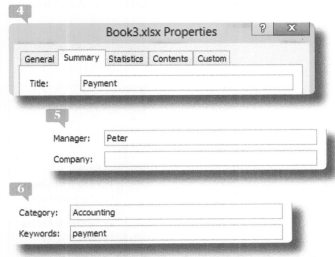

The **Summary** tab allows you to enter standard type properties for the document (title, author, manager, category, keywords, etc.). The **General**, **Statistics**, and **Contents** tabs, on the other hand, offer non-customizable information about the document.

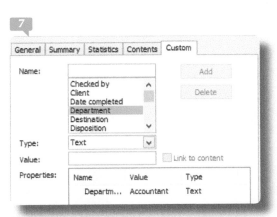

The **Custom** tab allows you to add new attributes such as department, office, registration, and end date, etc. When accepting the Properties window, the information is updated in the appropriate panel.

Saving a workbook

THE FIRST TIME YOU SAVE A WORKBOOK, Excel will prompt you for the name you want to give it and the location where you want it saved. Later on, once the save conditions have been set, the program will save the file in the same location and with the same name simply by clicking the Save icon.

1. In this exercise you will learn how to save an Excel workbook. Click on the **Save** tool, whose icon is displayed as a diskette in the **Quick Access Toolbar**.

2. This enables the **Save As** category of the redesigned **File** menu in which you must first specify where you wish to save the file. As a new feature in Excel 2013, you can select a cloud location, such as a SkyDrive storage space, and even add other sites, as you will see later on. In this case, click on the **Computer** option.

3. Your recent folders and the **Browse** button are now displayed, to allow you to select any other location that does not appear in the list. In this case, choose the **My Documents** folder.

4. This opens the **Save As** window, where you must specify the workbook's name and the format in which you want to save

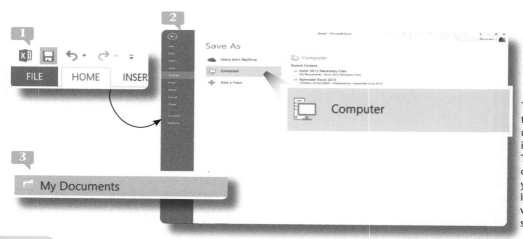

The first time you try to save a workbook using the Save icon in the **Quick Access Toolbar**, the Save As category, in which you must specify the location where the workbook will be saved, is enabled.

it. Enter a name for your file in the appropriate field and, keeping the **Excel Workbook (.xlsx)** file type selected, click on the **Save** button. 🔲

5. Once the workbook has been saved, if you make any changes to it and click on the **Save** function again, the **Save As** section will no longer appear, and it will save itself directly with the properties you set previously. Try it. Type **10** in the **C5** cell and press the **Enter** key to confirm it.

6. This time, click on the **File** tab and click on the **Save** option. 🔲

7. See what happens when you try to close a book with unsaved changes. Go to a cell with contents, press the **Delete** key to erase it, and click on the **X** button in the **Ribbon** to try to close it.

8. Excel asks you if you want to save the changes in this book. If you accept, the book will be saved with the latest settings, and, if you don't, the version prior to deleting the content will be kept. Click on the **Cancel** button in the Microsoft Excel window. 🔲

You can also directly access the **Save as** window using that option in the **File** menu. Thanks to this function you can save copies of the same document under different names and in different locations.

You will always find the Save and Save As options within the File tab. To run the Save function, you can also use the **Ctrl + S** shortcut.

If you try to close the workbook without having saved your changes, Excel will prompt you with this message.

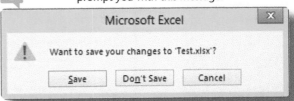

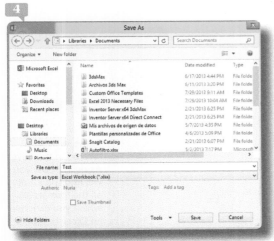

By default, the workbook is saved with the .xlsx extension, the Excel 2013 format in which the final x is a reference to Office **Open XML**.

Converting from Excel 97-2003 to Excel 2013

IMPORTANT

Remember that the usual .xls format for workbooks in versions previous to 2007 was replaced by the new **.xlsx** extension, while the format for .xlt templates changed to .xltx.

A WORKBOOK CREATED IN PREVIOUS VERSIONS of Excel (before Excel 2013), can be opened in this version of the program, and a workbook created with Excel 2013 can be saved in the format used in earlier versions. Similarly, when you open a workbook that has an Excel 97-2003 extension in Excel 2013, the Convert function is activated, which enables you to save it as .xlsx, which is the format for Excel 2013.

1. In this exercise you will learn how to save an Excel 97-2003 workbook in Excel 2013 and then convert it to an .xlsx format. Begin with an Excel workbook open in the application. Click on the **File** tab and select the **Save As** option.

2. In the **Save As** window, keep the field **Computer** selected and click on **My Documents**.

3. When the **Save As** dialog box opens, click on the arrow in the **Save as type** field, which shows the **Excel Workbook** option by default, and select **Excel 97-2003 Workbook**.

4. Remember that saving the document in this format creates two files with the same name, one with an **.xls** extension and the other with an **.xlsx** extension. Keep the name of the original workbook and click on the **Save** button.

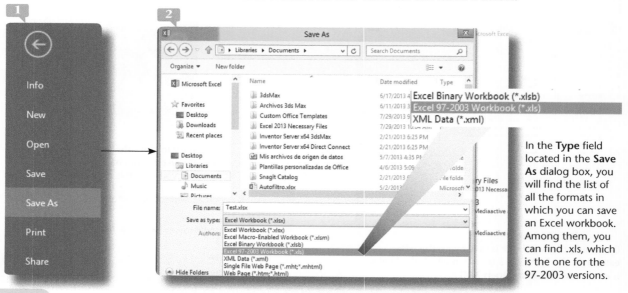

In the **Type** field located in the **Save As** dialog box, you will find the list of all the formats in which you can save an Excel workbook. Among them, you can find .xls, which is the one for the 97-2003 versions.

5. Look at the **Title Bar**. A new workbook has been created with the extension for Excel 97-2003 workbooks. When working with that type of workbook, you can change the format of the document back to Excel 2013 with the **Convert** option from the **Info** category on the **File** menu. 🔳[3]

6. As you can see, this option opens the **Save As** dialog box again in which the correct extension is already selected in the **Type** field. Since you already have this book in that format, you can cancel the dialog box. 🔳[4]

7. Click on the **X** button located on the **Title Bar** to close the workbook that has the extension .xls. 🔳[5]

As you can see, the steps you have to follow to save a file with a format from versions earlier to 2007 as an Excel 2013 workbook and to convert an .xls archive into an .xlsx archive are very simple. For this second case, remember that some new features in Excel 2013 may be disabled in order to avoid problems when working with earlier versions of Excel.

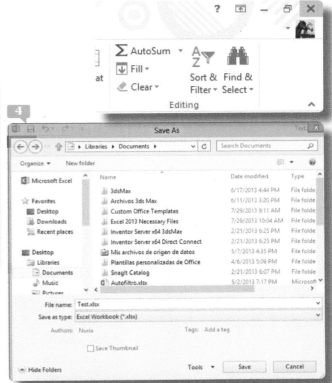

011

IMPORTANT

You can also change the file type from the **Export** category in the **File** menu.

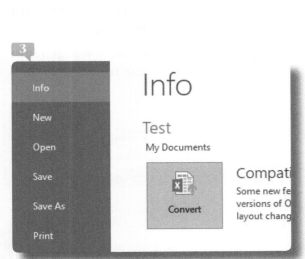

The **Convert** option allows you to save a file from an earlier version in the Excel 2007–2013 format, .xlsx.

Saving as PDF or XPS

THE PDF AND XPS FORMATS make the electronic publishing of Excel workbooks easy, and you can see what they will look like when printed. In order to save Excel workbooks in those formats just select the correct option in the Type file located in the Save As window.

1. Imagine you have to send the workbook that you are practicing on to several people so that they can correct it and add comments. Click on the **File** tab and select the **Save As** option.

2. Select the **Computer** field and the **My Documents** folder,  click on the arrow button in the **Save as type** field located in the window **Save As,** and select the **PDF** option.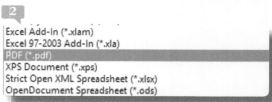

3. You will see several options related to the Adobe PDF format. If you keep the **Open file after publishing** option activated, the system will open the appropriate program to display the documents (Windows 8 Reader, Adobe Reader, or Adobe Acrobat) if it is installed on your computer. Click on the **Options** button that is located in the **Save As** dialog box.

4. In the **Options** window 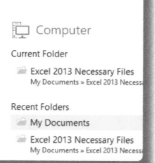 you can indicate the page range that you want to save, you can also choose to save the entire

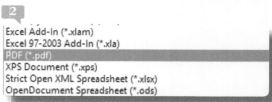

Save As

In the **Options** dialog box you can set the publishing requirements.

012

workbook or just a selection, and the type of non-printing information that you want to include, among other options. Keep the options as shown by default and click on the **OK** button.

5. Click on the **Save** button.

6. In a few seconds the PDF document is created and in this case, the **Windows Reader** (for Windows 8) opens and you can see the result of your work.  Place the cursor in the upper left-hand corner of the screen and click on the Desktop thumbnail to go back to the Excel Workbook window.

7. The steps you must take to save the same workbook in the XPS format are identical to the ones you have just seen. Go back to the **Save As** dialog box and select the **XPS Document** format 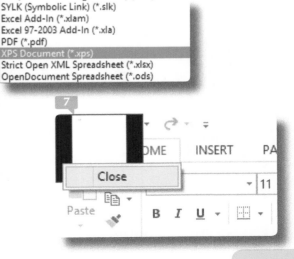 in the **Save as type** category.

8. Click on the **Save** button.

9. The file with an .xps extension that has been created can also be opened in the Windows Reader. Show the Excel workbook window again.

10. Place the cursor in the upper left-hand corner of the screen and use the **Close** option from the context menu on the reader's thumbnail to close it and finish the exercise.

IMPORTANT

The XPS format (XML Paper Specification) is Microsoft's alternative to the PDF format; it uses the XML technology that also facilitates document sharing (the exchange of documents).

Desktop

In Windows 8 the thumbnails of all open applications are hidden in this left side panel.

SYLK (Symbolic Link) (*.slk)
Excel Add-In (*.xlam)
Excel 97-2003 Add-In (*.xla)
PDF (*.pdf)
XPS Document (*.xps)
Strict Open XML Spreadsheet (*.xlsx)
OpenDocument Spreadsheet (*.ods)

Close

Once a document has been converted into a document in **PDF format**, you can open it with the new **Windows Reader**, with **Adobe Reader**, or with **Adobe Acrobat**.

Saving and sharing files online

IMPORTANT

If you have not logged in from your Office account, you will have to enter your log-in information in the corresponding window when activating the publishing function on SkyDrive.

ONE OF THE MOST INTERESTING INNOVATIONS in the whole Office 2013 suite is that it allows you to save the documents that you have created using its various applications to its own online storage location, such as SkyDrive, a free storage space, or the Office 365 service. This also allows users to easily share documents no matter what device they are using or where they are.

1. In this exercise you will see how to save an Excel workbook to the cloud in order to be able to access it at any time or from any place, therefore, making it easy to share it with other users. In this exercise, you will save the workbook to your SkyDrive storage place. In order to do this, you need an Office account and you must be logged in. Click on the **File** tab and click on the **Save As** option.

2. If you are logged into your Office account, your user name will show up next to the **SkyDrive** option. Click on that option.

3. The workbook will be stored both in your Internet space and in the SkyDrive documents folder on your computer so that you can work offline and that the changes are automatically synced when you connect to the service again. If the SkyDrive folder where you want to save your workbook does not show up in **Recent Folders**, use the **Browse** button to locate it.

Use the **Add a Place** option on the **Save As** pane in the Backstage view to add an Office 365 or another SkyDrive place.

4. When the **Save As** dialog box opens, select the folder you are looking for and choose a name and format for the workbook. Apply the changes and click on the **Save** button.

5. Now that the file has been saved on SkyDrive, see how you can share it with other users so that they can make alterations to it and you can therefore work on group projects. Click on the **File** tab and click on the **Share** category.

6. The name of the workbook that was published on the cloud is now showing in the Backstage view for this category. As you can see, you can now send an invitation to other users in order to share it with them, get a sharing link, post to social networks, or e-mail it. Keep the **Invite People** option enabled and write one of your contact's e-mail addresses in the first field.

7. You can specify if that user can only see the workbook or if he or she can alter it as well, and you can also add a personal message along with the invitation and ask the user to log on in order to be able to access the workbook. Click on the **Share** button.

After a few steps, check the **Shared with** field to make sure that you appear as the owner and that your contact shows up and has been given the sharing privileges that you had established.

013

IMPORTANT

In order to be able to share folders that have been published on the cloud on social networks (Facebook, Twitter, LinkedIn), your Microsoft account has to be connected to those networks.

Adding services to your Office account

IMPORTANT

Remember that if you have logged on to Office with a personal, company, or school account instead of a Microsoft account, the services you see on the **Add a service** button might be different.

ALSO NEW TO EXCEL 2013 is the possibility to add various services to your user account in order to add images and videos from your favorite places, store your documents on the cloud in order to access them at any time and from any location, and share them with your friends and acquaintances.

1. Microsoft Office 2013 lets you add services to the Office account you are working on, such as social networks (Facebook, Twitter, and LinkedIn), image and video publishing (Flickr and YouTube), storage in the cloud (Office 365 SharePoint and SkyDrive). Click the **File** tab and then click on the **Account** category. 🔲

2. In the Backstage view from that category, you can see and edit your user account information, find information about the version you are using, change some interface options such as the Office background, check what services are connected, and add new services. Click on the **Add a service** button. 🔲

3. As mentioned in the introduction, in this version of Excel you can connect to services that allow you to add pictures and videos from your Facebook, Flickr, and YouTube sites, store documents in the cloud with Office 365 or SkyDrive, and share documents with your Facebook, Twitter, and LinkedIn contacts. In order to be able to add those services you have to

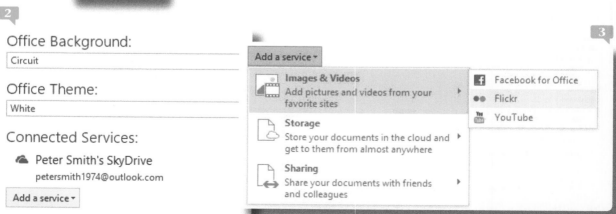

have accounts for each of them. Click the **Images & Videos** option and choose the **Flickr** command. [3]

4. A pop-up window appears and informs you about the action you are about to perform, the connection of your Flickr account with your Office account, which will allow you to view your photographs and videos that are published on this service in Office and other places from which you log in with your Microsoft account. Click the **Connect** button. [4]

5. You must now enter your Flickr user information. Enter it and then click on the **Sign In** button. [5]

6. The information on the window is updated to show that you are connected to Flickr. Click on the **Done** button.

7. Notice that the new service you have now connected to shows in the **Connected Services** section. Click on the **Manage** link. [6]

8. The browser opens and shows the page with your connection settings. From there you can customize the information that you want to share and you can also cut the connection altogether. Keep the **View your Flickr photos and videos** checkbox selected [7] and click on the **Save** button.

9. In the next window you can keep adding and managing accounts. Press the arrow button on your **Title Bar** to close the browser, go back to the Excel workbook, and finish the exercise.

From the Flickr log-in window you can also create a new account or sign in with your Facebook or Google accounts.

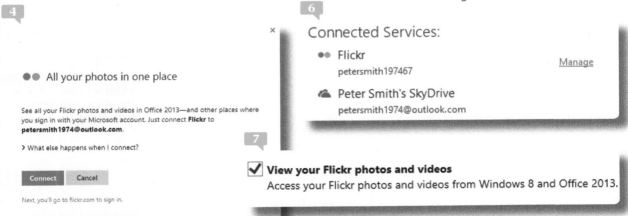

4

●● All your photos in one place

See all your Flickr photos and videos in Office 2013—and other places where you sign in with your Microsoft account. Just connect **Flickr** to **petersmith1974@outlook.com**.

> What else happens when I connect?

Connect   Cancel

Next, you'll go to flickr.com to sign in.

6

Connected Services:

●● Flickr
petersmith197467   Manage

☁ Peter Smith's SkyDrive
petersmith1974@outlook.com

7

✓ **View your Flickr photos and videos**
Access your Flickr photos and videos from Windows 8 and Office 2013.

Working with rows and columns

THE CELLS THAT MAKE UP a worksheet are organized into rows and columns. The columns are labeled alphabetically with a letter or group of letters located on top, and the rows are labeled numerically with a number located on the left. In this lesson you will learn how to select whole columns and rows.

1. In order to work with rows and columns you will take a file that contains data. Open the **Points.xlsx** workbook that you can download from our website.

2. Click on letter **C**, which labels the third column.

3. Any alterations that you might make at this point would affect all the cells in column C. Click on number **5**, which is located on the left side of the fifth row.

4. In order to select the whole worksheet, click on the gray square with an arrow, which is located at the intersection between the names of the first row and the first column.

5. The whole spreadsheet is selected now. In order to reverse this action, click on any cell.

1

	A	B	C	
1	Points	1 Game	2 Game	3
2	Álvarez		60	10
3	Pérez		35	50
4	Bonito		30	35
5	Flores		40	30
6	Vera		35	35
7	Balaguer		35	45
8	Asensi		20	15
9	Nerín		10	35

You can select whole rows and columns by clicking on their headings. When you select a row or a column, the changes will affect all cells.

2

	A	B	
1	Points	1 Game	2 Gam
2	Álvarez		60
3	Pérez		35
4	Bonito		30
5	Flores		40
6	Vera		35
7	Balaguer		35
8	Asensi		20
9	Nerín		10

In order to select the whole sheet, you have to press the arrow button that is located in the upper left-hand corner of the sheet. Deselect by clicking on any cell.

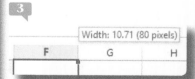

3

Width: 10.71 (80 pixels)

F	G	H

Left-click between two columns to see the width of the column located on the left.

015

6. By default, the columns have a set width of 80 pixels. You can customize this width. Place the cursor between the letters that are located in the column headers, and you will notice that its shape changes. Click with the left mouse button and hold it down in order to see the column width. ▣

7. The label tells you the column width. The rows have a preset height of 20 pixels or 15 characters, which can also be modified. Place the pointer between the numbers that label rows **6** and **7**, for example, and hold down the left mouse button to see the height of the row.

8. In order to change the standard size of a column, right-click on its header and select **Column Width** from the pop-up menu. ▣

9. In the **Column Width** window type **6**, for example, and click **OK** to apply the change. ▣

10. You will notice that the column is narrower now. In order to change the height of a row, right-click on its header and choose **Row Height** from the pop-up menu. ▣

11. In the **Row Height** window, type **18**, for example, and click the **OK** button. ▣

Click on the **Save** icon located on the **Quick Access Toolbar** in order to save the changes and finish the exercise.

IMPORTANT

You can also manually change the width and the height of the rows and columns. Place the cursor between two headers and when the shape of the cursor changes, click and drag to change the measurements.

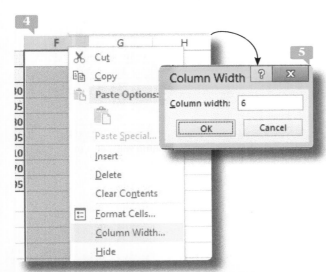

The pop-up menu located at the header of any column includes the **Column Width** option, which opens the Column Width dialog box that allows you to change the width of the selected column.

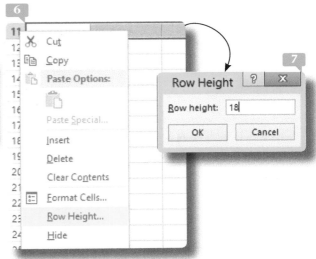

The pop-up menu located at the header of any row column includes the **Row Height** option, which opens the Row Height dialog box that allows you to change the height of the selected row.

Autofitting columns and rows

AUTOFITTING IS ANOTHER WAY to change the width of the columns and the height of the rows. Just as with the other related features, you can find the AutoFit feature by clicking on the Format button, in the Cells group on the Home tab.

1. In this exercise, you will see how to adjust the cells and the rows to fit the contents of some of the cells from the **Points** workbook that you used during the previous practice exercise. Select the C column and make sure that the contents of the cell C1 are longer than the column width. **1**

2. Click on the **Format** button located in the **Cells** group, on the **Home** tab, and click on the **AutoFit Column Width** option. **2**

3. The whole column widens automatically in order to display the whole contents that previously exceeded its default size. **3** Go back to the default size in order to perform the same action through another method. Click on the **Undo** icon **4** located on the **Quick Access Toolbar**.

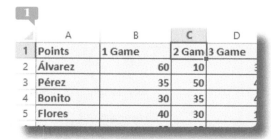

	A	B	C	D
1	Points	1 Game	2 Gam	3 Game
2	Álvarez		60	10
3	Pérez		35	50
4	Bonito		30	35
5	Flores		40	30

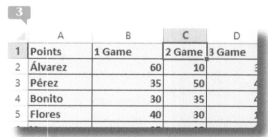

	A	B	C	D
1	Points	1 Game	2 Game	3 Game
2	Álvarez		60	10
3	Pérez		35	50
4	Bonito		30	35
5	Flores		40	30

All the cells that make up the column will adjust to fit the longer contents.

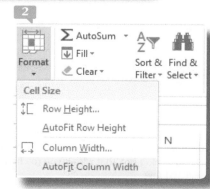

Use the **AutoFit Column Width** option by clicking on the **Format** button to increase or reduce the size of the selected column according to its contents.

You can use the **Undo** icon to cancel the last action you performed.

016

4. In order to adjust the width of the column to the longer contents again, double-click on the boundary located between the headers for this column and the next one.

5. The result is the same. The column adjusts to fit the longer contents. Click once more on the **Format** button, and this time choose the **Column Width** option.

6. In the **Column Width** window  that you had already worked with previously, type **10.21** and click **OK**.

7. You have to follow the same steps in order to AutoFit the height of the rows to fit their contents. Drag down the boundary below one of the row headers on your sheet in order to slightly increase its size.

8. Click on the header to select the whole row, then click on the **Format** button, and this time choose the **AutoFit Row Height** option.

9. This way, Excel adjusts the height of the selected row to fit its contents. In order to assign it a specific height again, you can use the **Row Height** window from the **Format** button or from its pop-up menu. In this case, you will leave the sheet as it is now and save the changes with the **Save** button on the **Quick Access Toolbar**.

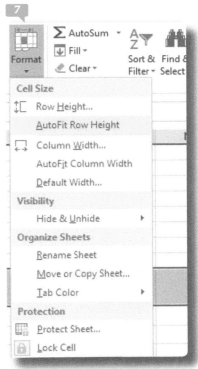

When you use the **AutoFit Row Height** option from the **Format** button, the height of the selected row will adjust to its highest content, and its size will be increased or reduced.

5

Column Width

Column width: 10,21

OK   Cancel

Access the **Column Width** window from the **Format** button in order to assign a specific width to the selected column.

You can manually change the default height of a row by dragging the boundary below it.

6

2	Álvarez	60	10	35
3	Pérez	35	50	45
4	Bonito	30	35	40
5	Flores	40	30	10
6	Vera	35	35	35
7	Balaguer	35	45	30
8	Asensi	20	15	35
9	Nerín	10	35	50
10				

Inserting rows, columns, and cells

IN ORDER TO ADD A ROW, A COLUMN, OR A CELL between existing ones, you must use the Insert command from the Cells group on the Home tab, or the pop-up menu for each of these elements. The number of columns or rows that you can insert at once will be the same as the number of columns or rows you had selected before using this feature.

1. In order to practice inserting files, columns, and cells, you will continue working with the **Points.xlsx** workbook. Select cell **A1** on your sheet and click the arrow button on the **Insert** command, which is in the **Cells** group, on the **Home** tab.

2. You can use this command to insert cells, columns, rows, and even sheets. Click on the **Insert Sheet Columns** option.

3. A column is inserted to the left of the selected one, and the **Insert Options** smart tag appears. Click on number **6** in the row header to select the whole row.

4. In this case, you would not use the **Insert Sheet Columns** because all the columns in this row are selected and you can- not increase their number. Click again on the arrow button located on the **Insert** tool and click on **Insert Sheet Rows**.

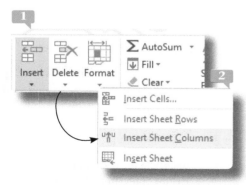

You will find the necessary features to insert cells, rows, columns, and sheets on the **Insert** button located in the **Cells** group.

	A	B	C	D
1		Points	1 Game	2 Gam
2		arez	60	
3		Pérez	35	
4		Bonito	30	
5		Flores	40	
6		Vera	35	
7		Balaguer	35	
8		Asensi	20	
9		Nerín	10	
10				
11				

If you want to insert multiple rows or columns at once, choose several of those before proceeding. The program will insert as many rows or columns as you have selected.

46

5. Select rows 2, 3, and 4. Click on the header for the second row, keep the **Shift** key pressed down and click on the header for row 4.

6. Right-click on the header for row 2 and a pop-up menu will appear, then, click on the **Insert** option from the pop-up menu. [5]

7. Three new rows are added, [6] which, depending on the option you have selected from the **Insert** options, will adopt the format of the row right above the first selected row. Click on cell **A1** to deselect.

8. You will now learn how to insert individual cells on the worksheet, between existing cells. Select cell **B11** for example.

9. Click again on the arrow button located on the **Insert** tool and click on the **Insert Cells** option.

10. When you insert an individual cell, the program cannot decide without your help if the cell will be inserted as part of a row or a column. From the **Insert** dialog box you can choose between shifting the cells right or down or also inserting a whole row or column. Keep the **Shift cells down** [7] option selected, and click **OK**.

11. Press the **Undo** icon located on the **Quick Access Toolbar** to undo the last action and save the file.

IMPORTANT

In order to quickly repeat the insert a column or a row action, click on the spot where you want to add the row or column and use the **CTRL + Y** shortcut.

When you insert a cell, the **Insert** dialog box allows you to choose where you want to insert that cell.

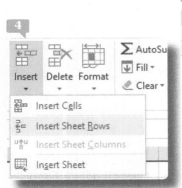

Select multiple rows from your sheet and use the **Insert** command to add the same amount of rows.

Three empty rows are inserted above the first row that you had selected.

Working with Insert Options

IMPORTANT

If you do not want the **Insert Options** smart tag to appear, disable **Show Insert Options buttons,** that you will find in the Advanced category in the Excel options dialog box.

- ☑ Show Paste Options button when cor
- ☑ Show Insert Options buttons
- ☑ Cut, copy, and sort inserted objects w

INSERT OPTIONS APPEAR ON THE SCREEN AS SMART TAGS, which offers you various options depending on whether you want to insert a column, a row, or a cell.

1. Select cell **A6** on the **Points.xlsx** file. Click on the arrow button located on the **Insert** tool, which is on the **Cells** group, and click on the **Insert Sheet Rows** option. 🗨

2. Automatically, a row is inserted above the selected one and the **Insert Options** tag appears. Click on it. 🗨

3. In this case, imagine you want the format for the new row to be the same as the row below it. Click on the **Format Same As Below** option button. 🗨

4. The inserted row will adopt the same characteristics and size as the row below it. You will now insert a new column. Select the whole column **C** by clicking on the letter located on its header.

5. Click on the arrow button on the **Insert** command and select the **Insert Sheet Columns** option.

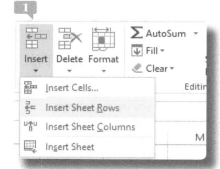

If a cell, a column, or a row has a custom format that is very different from the default one, you can use the **Insert Options** smart tag to copy this format into new inserted cells, rows, or columns.

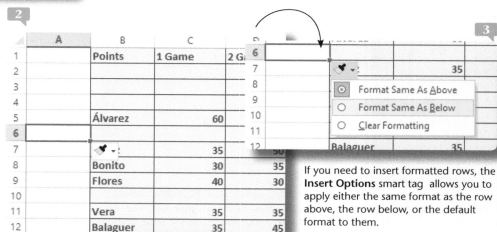

If you need to insert formatted rows, the **Insert Options** smart tag allows you to apply either the same format as the row above, the row below, or the default format to them.

6. A new column appears that has adopted the format as the one located to the left of the selected column. In this case, you want to adopt the size of the column located on the right as well as the format options that have been applied to it. Click on the **Insert Options** tag and select the **Format Same As Right** option.

7. Notice that the characteristics of the new column are the same as the column located on its right. Check to see if the data in the new column adopts the same format as well. Click on cell **C2**, type **10** and click on cell **A1** to check the result.

8. As you can see, the data you entered has aligned to the right. Insert a new cell. Click on cell **B10**, click on the arrow button located on the **Insert** command, and select the **Insert Cells** option.

9. Click on the **OK** button located in the **Insert** dialog box.

10. Click on the **Insert Options** tag and select **Clear Formatting**.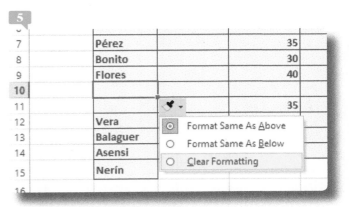

The cell is inserted without a default format. The **Insert Options** tag allows you to copy the format that you need or to simply insert an element that has the default characteristics set by the program.

You must use the **Insert** dialog box to indicate how the cells will shift when you insert a new one or if you want to insert a whole row or a whole column.

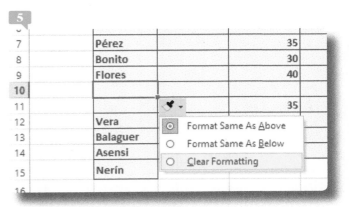

You have to select the **Clear Formatting** option on the Insert Options smart tag so that no specific formatting is applied to the rows, columns, or cells you insert, other than the Excel default formatting.

Deleting rows, columns, and cells

A ROW, A COLUMN, OR A CELL can be deleted from a spreadsheet, whether it is empty or it contains data. This action can be performed from the Delete command located in the Cells group on the Home tab after you have selected the part that is going to be deleted.

1. You will now see that the steps used to delete rows, columns, and cells are similar to those used to insert them. Keep on working with the **Points.xlsx** workbook. Click on the header for column **C** in order to select the whole column.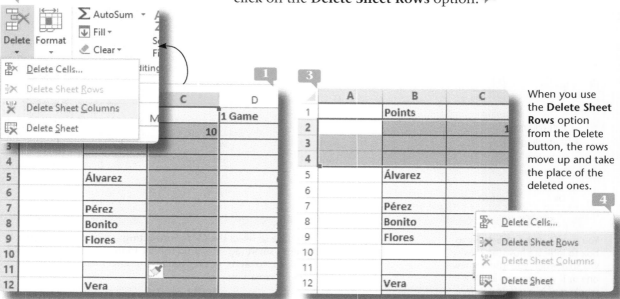

2. Pull down the **Delete** menu from the **Cells** group on the **Home** tab and select the **Delete Sheet Columns** option.

3. Column **D** has shifted to the left and taken the name and location of the deleted column. Since you don't want the column to disappear forever, press the **Ctrl + Z** shortcut to undo the last action.

4. Select row number **2**, and press and hold down the **Shift** key while you click on the header for row number **4**.

5. Pull down the **Delete** menu again, in the **Cells** group, and click on the **Delete Sheet Rows** option.

Select a whole row in your workbook and delete it by using the correct option from the **Delete** button located in the Cells group on the Home tab.

When you use the **Delete Sheet Rows** option from the Delete button, the rows move up and take the place of the deleted ones.

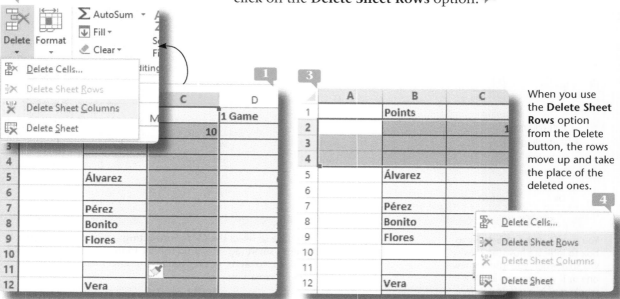

019

6. The lower rows move up and take the place of the deleted ones. You will now learn how to delete a cell. Select cell **B7** that you inserted during a previous exercise and which is now empty.

7. Click on the **Delete** arrow button and select the **Delete Cells** option.

8. The **Delete** dialog box will appear, which you must use to indicate whether the cells will shift right or up after being deleted or if you want to delete the whole row or the whole column where the selected cell is located. Select **Shift cells up** and click **OK**. 5

9. You can also delete rows, columns, and cells by using the corresponding option on its pop-up menu. Click on the header for row **3** in order to select the whole row.

10. Right-click on its heading and choose the **Delete** option from the pop-up menu that appears. 6

11. Delete all the empty rows, columns, and cells that you have inserted in the spreadsheet 7 and click the **Save** command on the **Quick Access Toolbar**.

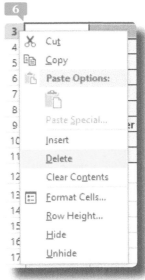

Just as you can insert rows, columns, and cells, you can also use the **Delete** option from their pop-up menus to delete them.

Make sure your spreadsheet looks the same as the one to the left, and that you have deleted the rows, cells, and columns that you had inserted into the spreadsheet.

When you delete a cell, the **Delete** dialog box appears, and you can use it to select where the cells will shift to or if you want to delete a whole row or column.

	A	B	C	D	E	F
1	Points		1 Game	2 Game	3 Game	Total
2	Álvarez		60	10	35	
3	Pérez		35	50	45	13
4	Bonito		30	35	40	10
5	Flores		40	30	10	8
6						
7	Vera		35	35	35	10
8	Balaguer		35	45	30	11

Hiding columns, rows, and sheets

IN THE FORMAT COMMAND FROM the Cells group you can find the Hide & Unhide function, which includes the necessary options to temporarily hide columns, rows, and sheets. Hiding those objects does not imply that their contents will be erased or will disappear from the sheet; it simply means that they do not show up when you view the worksheet.

1. In this exercise you will practice with the Hide rows, columns, and sheets function. You will keep on working with the **Points .xlsx** workbook. Imagine that you want to temporarily hide one of the sheets in your workbook. Put the cursor anywhere in the worksheet you want to hide, click on the arrow button from the **Format** tool in the **Cells** group, and place your mouse on the **Hide & Unhide** option.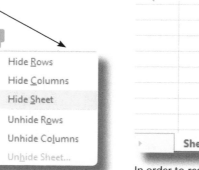

2. This option allows you to hide rows, columns, or sheets and then unhide them. Click the **Hide Sheet** option on the pop-up menu that appears on the screen.

3. The selected sheet has been hidden but not deleted. In order to restore it to view, you can either use the suitable option from the **Hide & Unhide** command located on the pop-up menu of the **Format** button or the **Unhide** option located in the sheet tabs pop-up menu. Right-click on one of the sheet tabs and select the **Unhide** option from the pop-up menu.

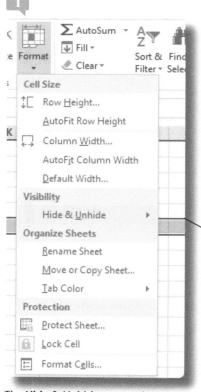

The **Hide & Unhide** rows, columns, and workbook sheets options can be found in the **Visibility** section on the **Format** drop-down menu.

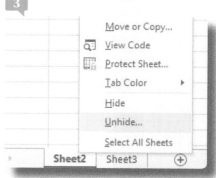

In order to restore a hidden sheet to view, use the **Unhide** option from the pop-up menu on the sheet tags.

4. The **Unhide** dialog box appears in which you have to choose the sheet that you want to unhide. In this case, since you have only hidden one sheet, select it from the dialog box and click the **OK** button.

5. You have to follow exactly the same steps in order to hide rows and columns. Select column **C** from your sheet for example by clicking on its header.

6. Click on the **Format** button, click on the **Hide & Unhide** option, and this time select the **Hide Columns** command.

7. Cell **C1** remains selected as you can see on the **Formula Bar**. Select column **B** by clicking on its header and click on the header for column **D** while holding down the **Shift** key.

8. Click again on the **Format** button, click on the **Hide & Unhide** command, and select the **Unhide Columns** option.

9. Column **C** is restored to view. You will do the same now with a row, but this time you will use its pop-up menu. Select row 6 by clicking on its header, right-click on it and select the **Hide** option.

10. To finish the exercise, you will restore the row to view. Select the row that comes before and the row that follows, rows **5** and **7,** and when you have selected them, right-click and select the **Unhide** option.

🔍	Find...
ᵃᵇₐ꜀	Replace...
→	Go To...
	Go To Special...

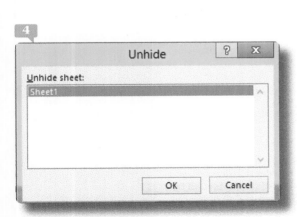

When you try to restore a hidden sheet to view, the **Unhide** dialog box opens up and you have to indicate which sheet you want to unhide.

In order to unhide hidden rows or columns, you first have to select the ones that come before and after and then use the **Unhide Rows** or the **Unhide Columns** options.

Hiding cells and windows

A HIDDEN CELL CAN STILL BE SEEN on the work area and on the printed sheet as well. Hiding a cell only hides the contents you see in the Formula Bar. The Hide window feature is only relevant when multiple windows of a same workbook are open.

1. In order to complete this exercise, you need to open two workbooks. You can use the **Points** workbook and the **Shopping list** workbook that we have generated from the same template name. Start by hiding a cell in the **Points** workbook. Select one that contains data, click on the **Format** button in the **Cells** group, and click on the **Format Cells** option. 🔲

2. Click on the **Protection** tab in the dialog box that opens, select the **Hidden** checkbox and click **OK**. 🔲

3. The feature doesn't appear to have any effect on the cell whose contents are still visible both on the sheet and in the **Formula Bar**. Click on the **Format** button once more and click on **Protect Sheet**. 🔲

4. You don't need to set a password, just click on the **OK** button in the **Protect Sheet** window.

5. The cell doesn't disappear, but its contents are no longer visible in the **Formula Bar**. Click on the **Format** button again

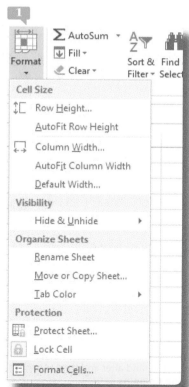

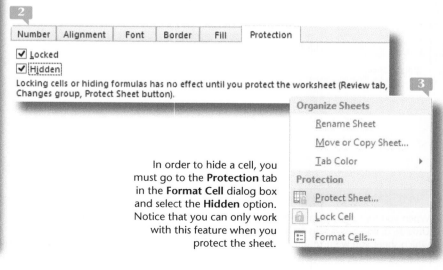

In order to hide a cell, you must go to the **Protection** tab in the **Format Cell** dialog box and select the **Hidden** option. Notice that you can only work with this feature when you protect the sheet.

021

and notice that while the worksheet is being protected the **Format Cells** option is not available.

6. You will now learn how to hide open windows. Go to **View** on the **Ribbon**.

7. Remember that you need to have more than one workbook open to perform this step. In order to hide the window that is now open, click the **Hide** button 🔲 in the **Window** group.

8. The inactive window is immediately hidden and you can now see the window of the second workbook you had opened. In order to unhide the hidden window, select the **View** tab and click on the **Unhide** button in the **Window** group. 🔲

9. The **Unhide** dialog box opens, 🔲 and you must select which workbook or workbook window you want to unhide. Select it and click on the **OK** button.

10. You will now learn how to view multiple open windows at the same time. Click on the **Arrange All** button in the **Window** group.

11. The **Arrange Windows** dialog box shows the different window positions available in Excel 2013. Select the **Horizontal** option, and click **OK**. 🔲

12. Try the other window positions and finish the exercise by maximizing one of them so that it shows in the foreground.

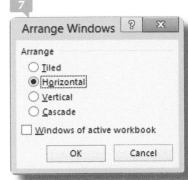

The **Arrange Windows** dialog box allows you to choose among the four window arrangements available in Excel 2013. Check and see what each of them does.

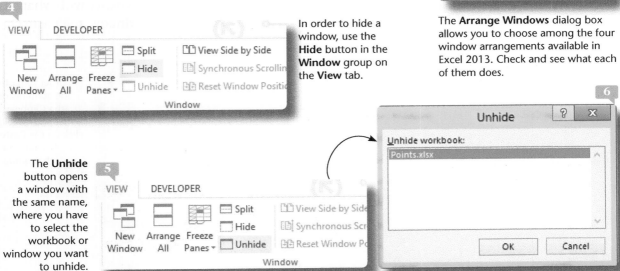

In order to hide a window, use the **Hide** button in the **Window** group on the **View** tab.

The **Unhide** button opens a window with the same name, where you have to select the workbook or window you want to unhide.

Copying, cutting, and pasting

IMPORTANT

Remember that the **Copy, Cut,** and **Paste** actions can also be performed by using the corresponding shortcuts **Ctrl + C, Ctrl + X,** and **Ctrl + V** as by using the selected item's pop-up menu.

THE EASIEST WAY TO COPY A CELL to an adjacent one is by dragging it by its lower right corner to its new cell. When you want to copy the cell to a cell located at the other end of the sheet or even onto another workbook, you have to use the Copy, Cut, and Paste commands. When you click one of the first two, the selected cell or range displays an outline of blinking dots, which indicates that its contents are on the Clipboard. You can insert the cell's contents over and over by clicking on the Paste button until it is removed from the Clipboard.

1. In this exercise you will learn about the cutting, copying, and pasting tools. Before you begin, unprotect the sheet from the **Points** workbook that you are going to work with if necessary. Select cell **C5**.

2. The copy, cut, and paste commands are located in the **Clipboard** group on the **Home** tab. Select this tab and click on the **Copy** command, which is the icon that looks like two sheets.

3. The dotted outline indicates that the contents of the cell are now on the Clipboard. The **Paste** tool is now activated as well. Select a blank cell as the target cell and click on the **Paste** tool in the **Clipboard** group.

4. When you use the **Paste** tool, and in accordance with what has been established in the **Excel Options** window, the **Paste** Op-

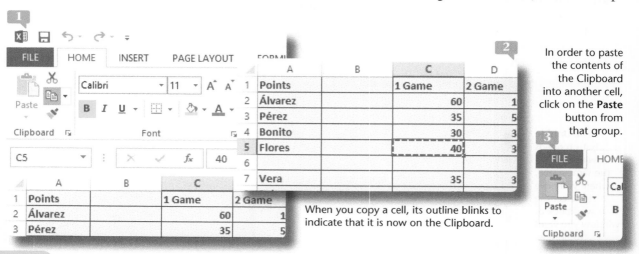

In order to paste the contents of the Clipboard into another cell, click on the **Paste** button from that group.

When you copy a cell, its outline blinks to indicate that it is now on the Clipboard.

tions smart tag will appear. You will practice with it in the next exercise. Select another blank cell and click on **Paste** again.

5. You can repeat the paste action as many times as you want as long as the copied cell remains on the Clipboard. In order to erase the contents of the Clipboard, press the **Escape** key.

6. Notice that the cell you copied does not display the blinking outline anymore and that the **Paste** tool is not available. You will now learn the difference between copying and cutting. Use the **Shift** key to select a cell range that contains data. 🔲

7. Click on the **Cut** button, which is the one that looks like scissors in the **Clipboard** group on the **Home** tab, 🔲 choose a blank cell as a target, and click on the **Paste** button.

8. As you can see, the **Cut** tool eliminates the contents of the selected cells and shows them in the cells that they are pasted in. You will now see what options are included in the **Paste** command. Select another cell that contains data and click on the **Copy** icon.

9. Select a target cell and click on the arrow which is under the **Paste** icon.

10. Depending on the copied contents, Excel lets you choose between pasting a formula, only the cell value, etc. If the cell you copied contains a formula, click on the **Formulas** option, 🔲 otherwise click on **Paste**.

11. Press the **Escape** key again to empty the **Clipboard** and save the changes you applied to the sheet before finishing the exercise.

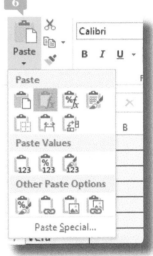

In order to find out the meaning of the **Paste** command options icons, place the mouse on one of them without clicking and a tag with the name of the option will appear.

30	35	40	105
40	30	10	80
35	35	35	105
35	45	30	110
20	15	35	70
10	35	50	95

You can also copy, cut, or paste a cell range. Remember that in order to select a range you have to use the **Shift** key.

The **Cut** icon in the Clipboard group is a pair of scissors.

Working with Paste options

THE PASTE OPTIONS SMART TAG appears next to the cells or ranges that have just been pasted. This tag, just like all the other smart tags in Excel, aims to make your work easier by displaying multiple options from which you can choose how you want to paste the copied or cut data.

1. Select a cell that contains some formatting from your sheet, for example the **Points** cell from the workbook that has the same name, and click on the **Copy** icon in the **Clipboard** group.

2. Choose the target cell and click on the **Paste** icon in the same group. 🔲

3. Notice that the **Paste Options** smart tag has appeared. Click on it to display all the available options.

4. Right now the selected option is **Paste**, which copies both the original format and its contents into the target cell. Click on the **Format** button, which is the first button in the **Other Paste Options** group. 🔲

5. The target cell looks empty because all you have copied from the source cell is the format. In order to check the result, just type **abc** and press the **Enter** key.

In order to discover the uses of the options included in the **Paste Options** smart tag, copy and paste cells that have a format, contain formulas, etc...

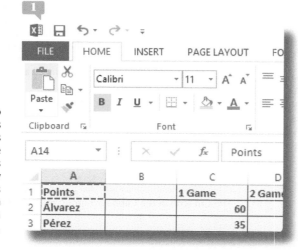

The **Format** option only applies the source cell format, not its contents.

6. The target cell now has the same characteristics as the source cell. You will now practice with another option displayed on the smart tag. Select a cell that contains a formula, any cell in the **Total** column, and click on the **Copy** button. 💬

7. Select the target cell and click on the **Paste** icon.

8. Click on the smart tag to uncover the pull-down menu with all the options and, if necessary, select the second icon from the second row of the **Paste** group, which corresponds to the **Keep Source Column Widths** option. 💬

9. The target cell adjusts its column width to match the width of the column of the source cell. Pull down the **Paste** options menu again and select the **Values** option, which is the first one in the **Paste Values** group. 💬

10. The target cell shows the same value as the source cell but not the same contents. Its contents are not the result of a formula, as they are in the source cell, they are simply a numeric value that you can see in the **Formula Bar**. Press the **Escape** key so that the smart tags disappear and save the changes you made by clicking on the **Save** button on the **Quick Access Toolbar**.

The **Keep Source Columns Widths** option applies the width of the column of the source cell to the column of the target cell.

	FILE	HOME	INSERT	PAGE LAYOUT	FORMULAS	DATA	REVIEW

F3		=SUM(C3:E3)

⁂	A	B	C	D	E	F
1	Points		1 Game	2 Game	3 Game	Total
2	Álvarez		60	10	35	
3	Pérez		35	50	45	130
4	Bonito		30	35	40	105

If you select and copy a cell that contains a formula, you can paste the whole formula into the target cell (which will adjust to the data that pertains to the new cell) or just the value it contains.

Finding and replacing data

A QUICK WAY TO ALTER DATA is by using the Find command and its assistant: the Replace command. These commands are particularly useful in very big spreadsheets with a large number of rows or columns, and they can both be found in the Find and Replace dialog box.

1. In this exercise you will learn how to find and replace data in a document. For that purpose, you will use a workbook with a lot of values. Click on the **Find & Select** command in the **Editing** group on the **Home** tab and click on the **Find** option.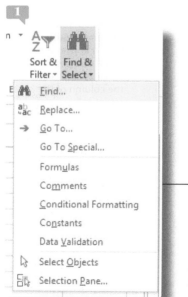

2. The **Find and Replace** dialog box will open and the **Find** tab will be selected. Imagine you want to find all the cells that contain a score of **35** for example. Type this value in the **Find what** field and click on the **Find Next** button.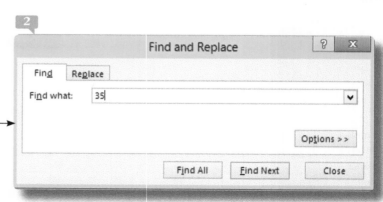

3. The first cell in the sheet whose contents match the ones you typed in is automatically selected. Keep clicking on the **Find Next** button to move on to the next matches.

4. Press the **Find All** button so that all the results of the search show in the window. Click on the **Close** button in order to close the window.

The **Find** option from the **Find & Select** drop-down menu opens up the **Find and Replace** dialog box, which allows us to perform bulk searches and replacements.

024

5. Imagine that you now have to replace one value for another. You can use the **Replace** command to avoid having to do it manually. Click on the **Find & Select** button again and click on **Replace**.

6. The program recalls the last search it performed. Imagine you have to change 35 to 25. Click into the **Replace with** field, type **25**, and click on **Replace**.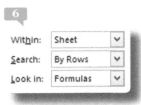

7. This way, the first 35 value is replaced with 25. In order to automatically replace all the rows, click on the **Replace All** button.

8. Notice that all the values have been replaced. Excel opens up an information box to let you know how many changes it made, so close it and click on the **OK** button.

9. Before closing the **Find and Replace** dialog box and finishing the exercise, look at the advanced search option available in Excel. Click the **Options** button.

10. Besides being able to determine the format of the cells that you want to find and replace, you can also specify what sheet you want to find them on or select the **Workbook** option from the **Within** drop-down menu, to look through all of its sheets. You can also search rows or columns and specify whether you want to find the cell's value or their underlying formulas. Hide the advanced search options by clicking on the **Options** button and close the **Find and Replace** dialog box by clicking on the **Close** button.

Within:	Sheet
Search:	By Rows
Look in:	Formulas

You can specify various search options in the **Find and Replace** dialog box by clicking on the **Options** button.

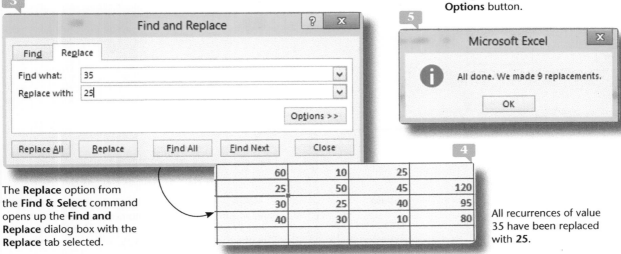

The **Replace** option from the **Find & Select** command opens up the **Find and Replace** dialog box with the **Replace** tab selected.

All recurrences of value 35 have been replaced with **25**.

Using different types of data

IMPORTANT

You can directly change the type of data that was entered in a cell, without having to use the **Format Cells** dialog box in the **Number** group on the **Home** tab of the **Ribbon**.

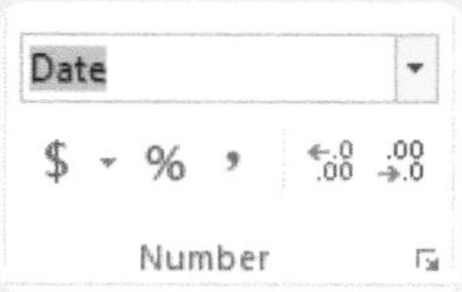

YOU CAN ENTER FORMULAS or fixed values into the cells in an Excel worksheet. The fixed values can also be text, numbers, or dates. Any data that is prefaced by an apostrophe is considered text, even if it is a numeric value or a mathematical formula.

1. In this exercise you will learn about the various kinds of data that can be entered into data cells. Select **Sheet2** in the **Points** workbook, select cell **B5**, type **house**, and press the **Enter** key.
2. By default, text is aligned left. Enter **15** in cell **B6** and press the **Enter** key.
3. Numbers are aligned right. Move up one cell by pressing the up arrow key.
4. You are now going to edit cell **B6** again. Click just before number **15** in the **Formula Bar**, press the apostrophe key, and then the **Enter** key.
5. The data you entered is now treated as text, and you cannot perform numeric calculations with it. Notice the green triangle that stands out in the upper-left corner of the cell. If you select that cell again, a tag with an exclamation point will pop

1

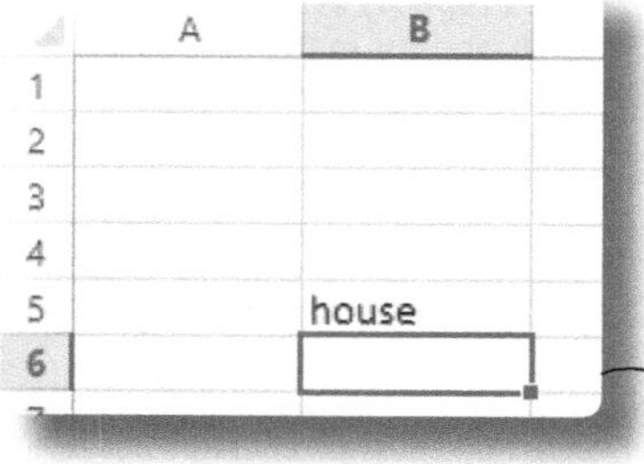

2

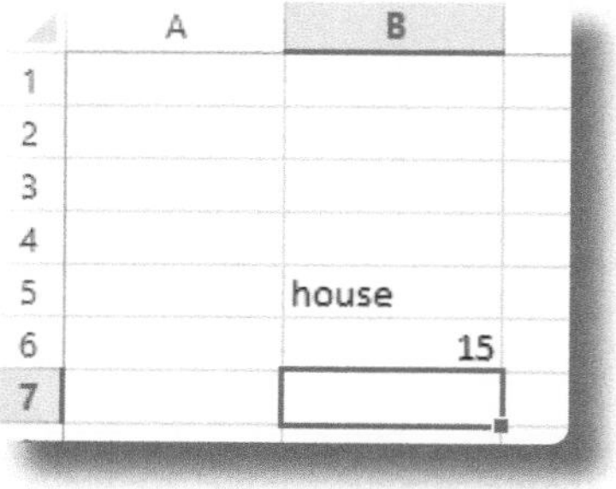

Text aligns left in the cell and numbers align right by default.

3

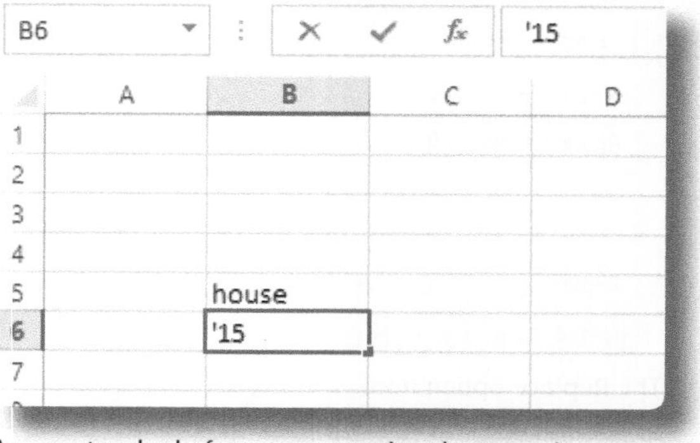

An apostrophe before any numeric value turns it into a text value that you will not be able to perform mathematical calculations with.

025

up: it is the tag that checks errors in the data that has been entered in the cells. Select cell **B6**, place the cursor on the error checking tab, read the message, and click on its icon to check all the available options.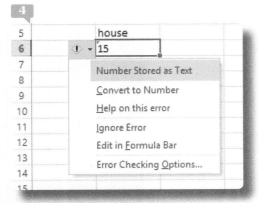

6. Click on the tag again to close the drop-down menu.

7. You will now see how Excel works with dates. Select cell **B7**, enter **25**, and press **Enter** in the **Formula Bar**.

8. Click on the **Format** button in the **Cells** group on the **Home** tab if the **Ribbon**.

9. This menu allows you to alter the size of the cells, to hide and unhide them, to arrange the sheets, and to set protection options for them. Click on the **Format Cells** option.

10. The **Format Cells** dialog box opens and the last tab you used is selected. Click on the **Number** tab, select **Date** from the categories list, choose one of the available formats and click **OK**.

As you can see, the dates are also aligned right in the cell by default, as if they were a numeric value.

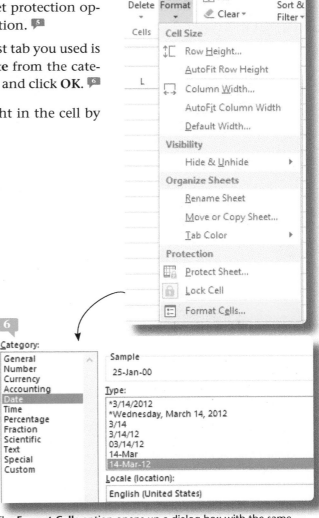

When a cell number is formatted as text or is preceded by an apostrophe, a tag appears that includes an options menu that allows you to convert the value to a number once and for all or to ignore the error.

The **Format Cells** option opens up a dialog box with the same name from which you can, among other options, alter the type of data you entered in a cell.

Editing and erasing data

IF YOU SELECT A CELL WITH DATA and you type again on the keyboard, the new data is written over the old data and replaces it completely. In order to add text to a cell that already contains the same kind of data without deleting it, you have to edit it.

1. Even though you learned how to enter data in previous lessons, you will continue practicing entering data in this exercise. Click on cell **B5** to select it. 1

2. If you entered new text right at this moment by using the keyboard, this text would completely replace the existing text. In order to edit the contents without deleting them, you have to open or edit the cell. Double-click on the cell, at the end of the word that is written in it. 2

3. The text cursor is placed on the spot where you clicked. At this point, the cell behaves as a text box and you can move around with the arrow located on the keyboard or delete letters with the **Delete** key. Click on the **space bar**, type **new,** and press **Enter** so that the action takes effect. 3

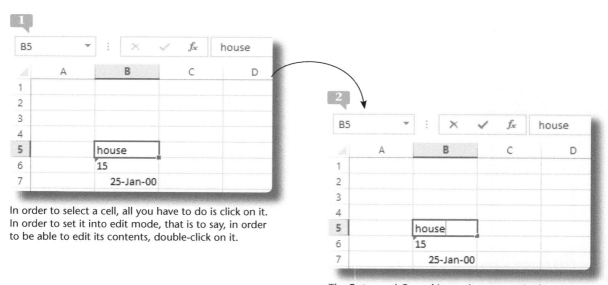

In order to select a cell, all you have to do is click on it. In order to set it into edit mode, that is to say, in order to be able to edit its contents, double-click on it.

The **Enter** and **Cancel** icons that appear in the **Formula Bar**, indicate that the selected cell is in editing mode.

4. Place yourself again on cell **B5** by clicking on it.

5. The **F2** key also edits the cell and places the text cursor at the end of the existing text. Another way to edit the cell is to place the cursor in the Formula Bar, at the exact spot where you want to make the change. Click before the word **new** in the **Formula Bar**.

6. Delete **new**, click before **house**, type **old**, click on **space bar**, and press the **Enter** key.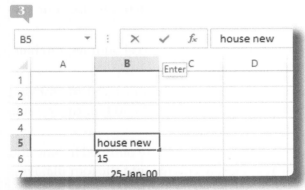

7. There is another way you can clear the contents of a cell. Right-click on cell **B7**.

8. From the drop-down menu that opens, select the **Clear Contents** option by clicking on it. The value that was in the selected cell disappears automatically.

IMPORTANT

In order to start a new line of text in a specific spot in a cell, click on the spot where you want to end the line and then press **ALT + Enter**.

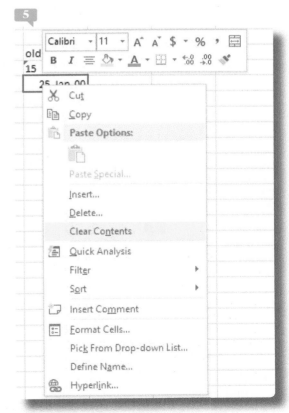

When you edit a cell, you can keep your changes by pressing the **Enter** key, in which case the cell right below will be selected according to the default properties of the program. Or, you can click on the **Enter** icon in the **Formula Bar**, in which case the cell you are editing will remain selected.

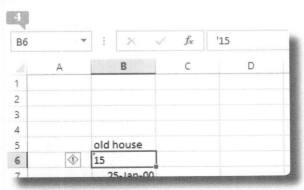

The **Clear Contents** option from the drop-down menu deletes all the contents in the cell.

Entering and editing formulas

FORMULAS ARE ESSENTIAL ITEMS on a spreadsheet. By entering them in the cells, you turn the sheet into a calculator that refreshes the results every time a variable is changed.

1. Since Excel 2010, writing formulas has been easier thanks to the resizable **Formula Bar** and the **AutoComplete** function. Select cell **C8**, type the following formula, **=5+6** 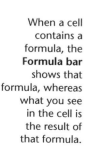 and click on the **Enter** button.

2. The program shows the cell and the result of the calculation, but in the **Formula bar** you can see the real contents of cell **C8**. Click to select cell **C10**.

3. In the selected cell, you will enter a formula with cell **C8** as its cell reference. Click in the **Formula bar** and use your keyboard to enter the formula =5+C8.

4. When you type cell **C8** as a reference, Excel outlines it in blue. Click on the **Enter** button.

5. The asterisk sign is used for multiplications and the forward slash is used for divisions. Select cell **C12** and type the formula **=C8*C10**.

6. The two cells that are referenced here are outlined in blue and red respectively when they are entered into the formula. Press on the **Enter** key and select cell **C12** again.

Formulas can be entered directly into the cell or in the **Formula Bar** and must always be preceded by the = sign which identifies them as such.

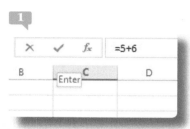

When a cell contains a formula, the **Formula bar** shows that formula, whereas what you see in the cell is the result of that formula.

7. As you can see, the cell shows the result of the multiplication while the **Formula Bar** shows the formula you entered. In cell **A1** type the formula **=5+6**.

8. Select cell **A3** and enter the formula **=10+A1**, press **Enter** and then enter the formula **=A1*A3** in cell **A4**, and press the **Enter** key again.

9. To make the example clearer, delete the contents of the **B5** to **C12** cell range. Use the **Shift** key to select the range and then press the **Delete** key.

10. There are different ways you can edit the formulas. Double-click on cell **A1**, press the **Backspace** key to erase number **6**, and type **3**.

11. Click the **Enter** button and see the changes that are made in all the cells that contain formulas with cell **A1**.

12. Now you will see a different way to edit formulas. Select cell **A3**, place the cursor right before the cell **A1** reference in the **Formula Bar**, delete this reference by pressing the **Delete** key twice, and select cell **A2**.

13. Press the **Enter** key to confirm the changes.

14. Since cell **A2** is empty, the result of the function will change, because the numeric value of an empty cell is equal to 0. Select cell A3, press the **Delete** key to clear all its contents, and save the changes by clicking on the **Save** icon in the **Quick Access Toolbar**.

IMPORTANT

When you enter the name of a cell in a formula, you are indicating that the formula will be calculated according to the contents of that cell. If the contents change, Excel will recalculate.

When a formula refers to several cells, each of them is outlined in a different color.

Creating and using lists

A LIST IS A SERIES OF WORDS OR NUMBERS that are interrelated and follow a set sequence. When you just enter one of these words in a cell, Excel recognizes it as being part of a list and it can keep filling the cells. The only lists that the program includes by default are the ones composed of the days of the week and the months of the year.

1. In this exercise, you will add a new custom list to the ones that already exist. Imagine you work for a restaurant and you need to draw up a daily menu for your restaurant. Click on the **File** tab and click on the **Options** command.

2. The **Excel Options** dialog box opens up, which you can use to configure the program according to your preferences. Select the **Advanced** category, click on the vertical scroll bar, go to the **General** section, and click on the **Edit Custom Lists**.

3. You can manually add new lists or import them from a specific selection of cells into the **Custom Lists** window. In the **List entries** box, type **First course**, **Main course**, **Dessert** (separate them with commas) as parts of the new list and click on the **Add** button.

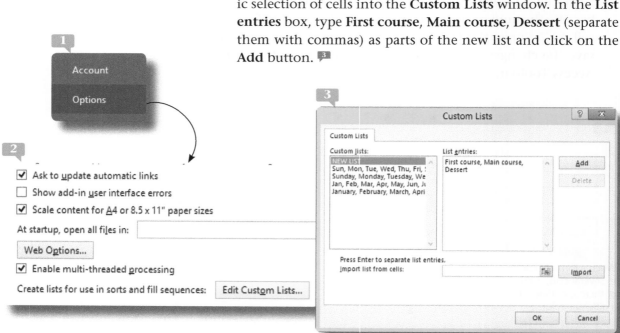

Access the **Custom Lists** box from the **Advanced** tab in the Excel Options window to create and manage your own lists.

028

4. The list you created is added to the **Custom lists** box. You can also create a list from a range of existing cells. In that same **Custom lists** box, click on the icon located to the left of the **Import** button.

5. The dialog box is now minimized. Select a range of cells with some contents (for example, the list of names from Sheet1 in the **Points** workbook) and when its name shows up in the minimized dialog box click on the icon located on the right of the text box.

6. Click on the **Import** button and notice that a new list has been created.

7. Now you will practice with the **First course, Main course, Dessert** list. Select it from the **Custom lists** box and click on the **OK** button.

8. Click **OK** in the **Excel Options** box.

9. Click in cell **A11**, type **First course** and press the **Enter** key to confirm the entry.

10. Click and select cell **A11**, click in the square located in its lower right corner, and, without releasing the mouse button, drag it down until cells **A12** and **A13** are also selected.

11. The program has filled the selected cells with the following items from the list. To finish, click on any cell to deselect the present selection.

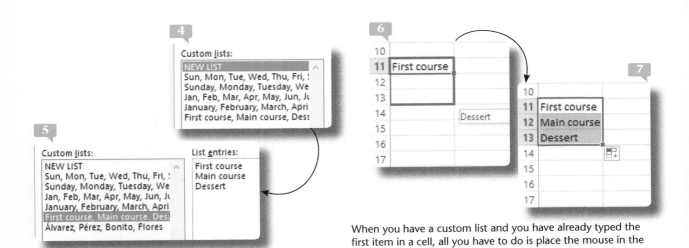

Custom lists work on an Excel sheet even if they are not selected in this box.

When you have a custom list and you have already typed the first item in a cell, all you have to do is place the mouse in the lower right corner of that cell and drag until you cover all the cells you want to complete.

Working with Auto Fill Options

THE AUTO FILL OPTIONS TAG APPEARS when you fill out a list automatically, and it allows you to edit the conditions for the Auto Fill you just performed. The options included are: Copy cells, Fill series, Fill formatting only, Fill without formatting, Fill (custom list), and Flash fill. This last option is one of the new features in Excel 2013 and it will be explained in the next exercise.

1. In order to work with the **Auto Fill** options, open a blank sheet in your workbook. Insert 3 in cell **A1**, press the **Enter** key, enter 4 in cell **A2**, and press **Enter** again.

2. Select cell **A1**, press and hold down the **Shift** key while you click on **A2** to select that range. 1

3. Go to the **Home** tab on the **Ribbon** and click on the **Center** tool icon, which is the second one on the second line of tools in the **Alignment** group. 2

4. The contents of both cells are centered. You will now fill this series automatically. Click in the square located in the lowe right corner of the two selected cells and drag it to cell **A6**. 3

5. At this point, the **Auto Fill Options** smart tag appears. In this case, the program has interpreted the list as a series of con-

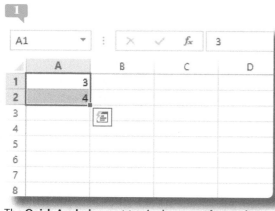

The **Quick Analysis** smart tag is also a new feature in Excel 2013, and it allows you to quickly turn data into charts or tables.

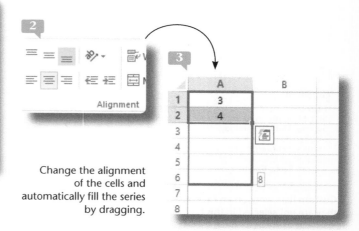

Change the alignment of the cells and automatically fill the series by dragging.

029

secutive numbers, but imagine you only wanted to copy the contents of the first two cells. Click on the smart tag and click on the **Copy Cells** option.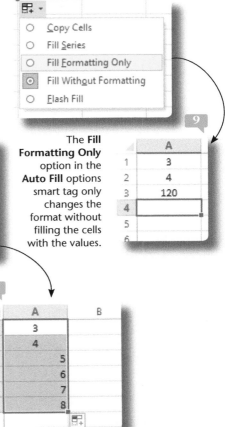

6. The contents of the filled cells have changed and you now see the exact copy of the two original cells including their format. The remaining options relate to the different fill options for a series. Imagine now that you want to fill this series without copying the format, so that the automatically filled cells are not aligned right, which is the default alignment for numeric values. Click on the **Auto Fill Options** smart tag and select the **Fill Without Formatting** option.

7. The contents of the filled cells are not copies of the original ones, they now contain a series of numbers with the Excel default alignment. You will now try to copy just the format, without any values. Click on the **Auto Fill** options again and select the **Fill Formatting Only** option.

8. At this point, the cells included between **A3** and **A6** are empty, but they have a centered alignment. This way, the data that you enter in any of the cells will adopt that alignment. Check this by typing **120** in cell **A3**.

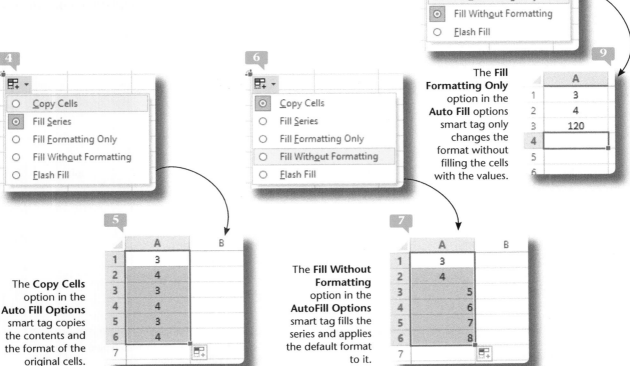

The **Copy Cells** option in the **Auto Fill Options** smart tag copies the contents and the format of the original cells.

The **Fill Without Formatting** option in the **AutoFill Options** smart tag fills the series and applies the default format to it.

The **Fill Formatting Only** option in the **Auto Fill** options smart tag only changes the format without filling the cells with the values.

71

Using the Flash Fill Tool

THE NEW FLASH FILL OPTIONS TAG WORKS as a data assistant that recognizes a pattern on the sheet and uses if to fill a series. It is particularly useful to split data columns as you will see in this exercise.

1. In this example you will use a list of first names and last names that you have entered in column A; imagine you want to split this data into independent columns. The new **Flash Fill Options** tool in Excel 2013 will allow you to do that quickly and easily. In **B1**, type the name of the first item from the list 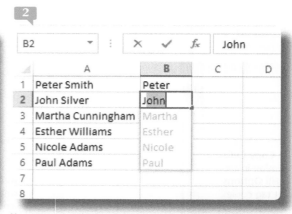 and press the **Enter** key.

2. Now start typing the name of the second item and notice how Excel shows a list of possible options using the names in the first column as a pattern. Press the **Enter** key to confirm the entry of this second item.

3. Column **B** is automatically filled with the corresponding first names and the new **Flash Fill Options** tag appears. Click on it.

Remember that the new Excel 2013 **Flash Fill** option is case sensitive.

You can press the **Escape** key to keep typing without using the **Flash Fill** suggestions.

4. This tag contains the options that allow you to undo Flash Fill, accept suggestions, and select blank cells and edited cells. Select the **Accept suggestions** option.

5. You will fill in the next column the same way, with the last names from your list. In cell **C1**, type the first last name from your list and click **Enter**.

6. Start typing the second last name; press **Enter** when the list of suggested names comes up, and in the **Flash Fill Options** smart tag, select the **Accept suggestions** option.

7. Remember that the new Flash Fill tool only works when the program recognizes a somehow coherent data pattern. That data does not have to be names. Flash Fill is also case sensitive therefore it can also be used to change the type of text (for example, a list of items in lowercase can easily be turned into a list in capital letters). To finish this exercise, you will learn how to disable the **Flash Fill Options** smart tag. Click on the **File** tab and click **Options**.

8. Select the **Advanced** category and notice that the **Automatically Flash Fill** option is checked by default. If you wish to disable it, click its check box and accept the changes.

030

IMPORTANT

You can also activate the **Flash Fill** tool from the **Data Tools** group on the **Data** tab or by clicking the **Ctrl + E** shortcut.

Text to Columns	Flash Fill	Remove Duplicates

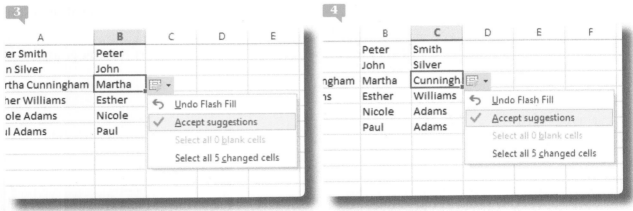

In case the **Flash Fill Options** utility does not recognize the pattern and does not let you fill in the data, you can always use the **Text to columns** tool to split text into different cells.

Sorting data

THE SORT FEATURE ALLOWS you to deal with issues that may arise when you are working with tables containing large amounts of rows that have been entered without a specific order. The order will be assigned based on numerical or alphabetical criteria, depending on the contents of the selected column. You have two options when sorting: ascending or descending.

1. For this exercise, you we will use the **Points2.xlsx** workbook, an edited version of the **Points** file into which you have reorganized the contents of Sheet1 in order to show the complete data table again. The **Sort** tools are located in the **Editing** group on the **Home** tab and in the **Sort & Filter** group on the **Data** tab. You will now arrange the list of names alphabetically. 🗨

2. Click on the **Sort & Filter** group button and click the **Sort A to Z** option. 🗨

3. The letters of the names serve as order criteria to automatically sort the whole table. 🗨 You will now sort the names alphabetically in descending order. In this case, you will be using the sorting tools on the **Data** tab.

4. Click on the **Sort Z to A** icon in the **Sort & Filter** group. 🗨

1

	A	B	C
1	POINTS	1 Game	2 Game
2	Flores	40	
3	Asensi	20	
4	Bonito	25	
5	Vera	60	
6	Balaguer	25	
7	Nerín	30	
8	Pérez	25	
9	Álvarez	10	

Select a cell from the column you want to sort, select the sort option you prefer from the **Sort & Filter** command, and notice how Excel carries out the action right away.

2

um

Sort & Find &
Filter Select

Editi A↓ Sort A to Z
       Z↓ Sort Z to A
       ⬆ Custom Sort...
       ▼ Filter
       ▼ Clear
       ▼ Reapply

3

	A	B	C
1	POINTS	1 Game	2 Game
2	Álvarez	10	
3	Asensi	20	
4	Balaguer	25	
5	Bonito	25	
6	Flores	40	
7	Nerín	30	
8	Pérez	25	
9	Vera	60	

031

5. Imagine that you want to sort the table so that it first shows the names with the lowest figures (points, height, etc.) and end with the ones with the largest figures. Click on the **Sort** tool from the **Sort & Filter** group.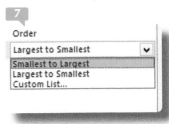

6. The **Sort** dialog box opens, and this is where you have to define the sorting criteria. Click on the arrow button in the **Sort by** field and select the **Total** column, which is where the values that you are going to sort are located.

7. Click on the arrow button in the **Sort On** field to see what options are available.

8. If you applied either manual or conditional formatting to a range of cells or a chart column, Excel allows you to sort them by cell color or font, or by cell icon. Keep the **Values** option selected.

9. Select the **Smallest to Largest** option in the **Order** field and press the **OK** button.

Remember that you can add up to 64 sorting levels by using the **Add Level** button in the **Sort** dialog box. Also, the Sort Options dialog box lets you choose the case and orientation.

You can find the **Sort & Filter** commands on the **Home** tab as well as on the **Data** tab.

The **Sort** button opens the dialog box of the same name from which you can define a number of criteria and sorting levels. Choose the column you want to sort, the kind of data it contains, and the sorting criteria.

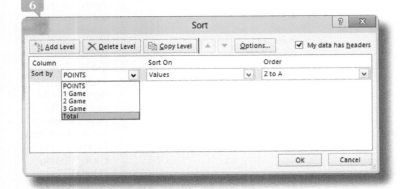

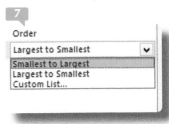

Notice that the values of the **Total** column have been sorted from smallest to largest.

Using AutoFilters

FILTERS ARE THE MOST USEFUL FUNCTION to help you locate rows that meet certain criteria and hide the ones that you do not want to view.

1. For this exercise, you will use a new book as an example. Download the **Autofilter.xlsx** document from our website, save it on your computer, open it, and select Sheet1.

2. As you can see, this spreadsheet is only made up of two columns, one that shows the months of the year and another one that shows the expenses incurred for each of these months. Click on cell **A1** to select it.

3. On the **Data** tab, click on the **Filter** 🗩 command in the **Sort & Filter** group.

4. In each of the cells that the program has interpreted to be labels, there is now an arrow button. Click on the arrow button that has appeared in the **MONTHS** header. 🗩

5. **AutoFilter** allows you to select items from a list of text values, to sort them, or to create criteria. Go to the list of months,

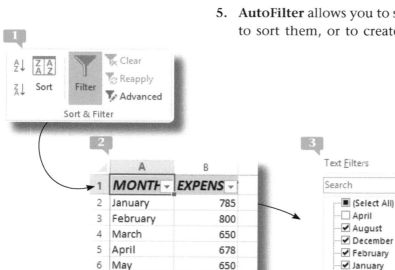

Apply the filter to the selected text cells and see what filtering options are available in Excel 2013. Choose several items in the list and apply the filter. See what the available **Text Filters** are and create filtering criteria.

uncheck the boxes for the months of **April**, **June**, and **March**, and press the **OK** button. 3

6. Those months do not show on the list anymore and the row numbers to the far left have turned blue, which tells you that a filter has been applied to them. In order to display all the months again, click on the arrow in the **MONTHS** header, check the **Select All** option box, and click **OK**. 4

7. You will now apply a number filter to column **B**. Click on the arrow button in the **EXPENSES** header and click on the **Number Filter** option to see what options are available.

8. You can use comparison operators (equal to, greater than, between, etc.) to establish some criteria or create your own custom filter. Select the **Between** option. 5

9. The **Custom AutoFilter** dialog box opens, which is where you have to enter the criteria to be applied by the filter. In this case, you are only going to display the values between 600 and 800. Click in the **is greater than or equal to** field and type **600**.

10. Click in the **is less than or equal to** field, type **800**, and click the **OK** button to apply the filter. 6

11. Notice that the list is updated and only shows the months with expenses that match the filter you applied. You will now remove the filter. Press the **Clear** command in the **Sort & Filter** tool group. 7

12. Click on the **Filter** command of the same group to remove the cell filter.

032

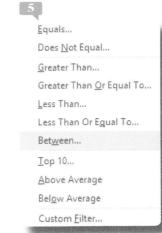

When you select the **Select All** option, all the items show again.

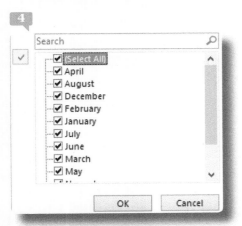

Select one of the default filtering criteria and you will access the **Custom AutoFilter**, where you will be able to set the filtering values.

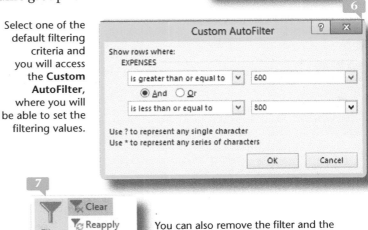

You can also remove the filter and the present order of the data range by using the **Clear** button. In order to remove the filter, click the **Filter** button.

Importing data from Access

IMPORTANT

In some cases, when you import data, you might need a password or some other kind of information to access the data. Since Excel 2010, there has been an **Excel Connections** manager that allows you to see all the connections for a workbook and makes it easier to reuse one of them or to substitute one for another.

THE IMPORT DATA TOOLS ARE LOCATED in the Get External Data group, in the Data tab, on the Options Ribbon. These tools allow you to import data from an Access database, from a web page, from a text file, or from other data sources that are included in the From Other Sources command.

1. You are going to import the data from an Access database. You already know the name of the data source file that you want to import as well as where you want to place it. If you do not have any Access documents, download **ChildrensBooks. accbd** from our website and save it to your computer. Select a blank Excel page.

2. Select the **Data** tab on the **Ribbon** and click on the **From Access** button in the **Get External Data** group.

3. Use the **Select Data Source** dialog box to locate and open the folder containing the Access file with all the data you want to import. Select it and click on the **Open** button.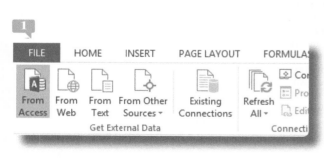

4. If the database is made up of several tables, as it is the case in this example, the **Select Table** dialog box opens up from

Locate and select the database file you want to import to Excel by using the **Select Data Source** dialog box.

033

which you have to select the chart that you want to import. Select the one named **Children's Books1** and click the **OK** button.

5. You have to use the **Import Data** dialog box to define how the data will display in the book as well as the exact spot in the present sheet or in a new one, where it will be placed. In this case, you will keep the **Table** option selected so that the data shows as a table and you will also keep cell **A1** from the present spreadsheet selected so that the chart is placed in that spot in the workbook. Before you accept importing the table data, take a look at what its properties are. Click on the **Properties** button.

6. In the **Connections Properties**, click the **Refresh every** option checkbox.

7. When you edit the data in the database, it will be updated on the spreadsheet every 60 minutes, which is the default established time. Click on the **OK** button.

8. Click the **OK** button in the **Import Data** dialog box so that the data range is imported directly to the selected sheet.

Now the table has been added to the selected sheet, in the spot that you had chosen. Simultaneously, the **Table Tools** tab appears in the **Ribbon** and you can use its improved design tools to edit the appearance of the table.

In the **Import Data** dialog box, indicate how you want to view the data in the workbook and where you want to place it. If you want to see the properties of the database, click the **Properties** button.

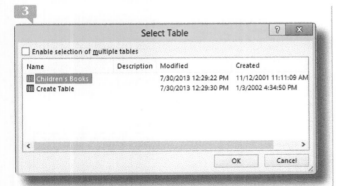

If your database contains more than one table, you will have to use the **Select Table** dialog box to select the ones that you want to import. Otherwise, the **Import Data** dialog box will open.

Importing data from text

IMPORTING DATA FROM TEXT is achieved the same way as importing Access data. In this exercise you will import a text document to the same page of the workbook that you used in the previous exercise.

1. Select an empty cell, **A22** for example.

2. Select the **Data** tab on the **Ribbon** and press the **From Text** button in the **Get External Data** group.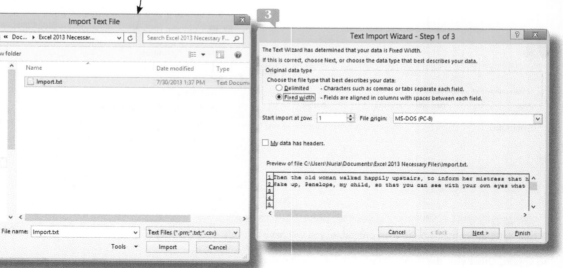

3. The **Import Text File** dialog box opens, and, by default, shows the contents of the **Documents** folder. Locate the folder that contains the text file you want to import. (If you do not have any .txt files, you can download the one called **Import.txt** from our website.)

4. Select the text file and click the **Import** button.

5. When you import a text document, the **Import Text Wizard** opens, which lets you define how you want to import your text in three steps. You can use the **Preview of file** section to see what your document will look like when you import it to the spreadsheet. Keep the default settings as they appear in the first step of the Wizard and click **Next**.

034

6. The next screen allows you to set the width of the fields. Click **Next** to save the default width.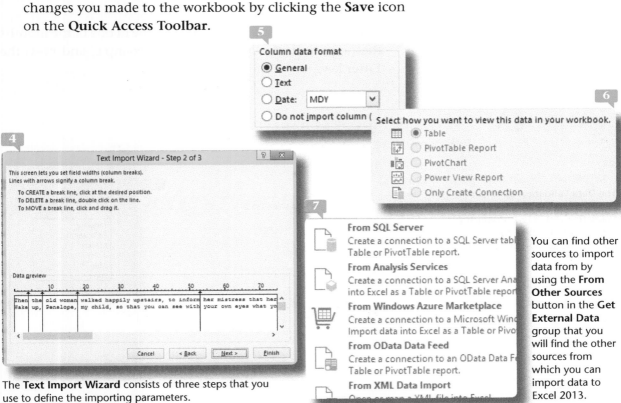

7. The last screen lets you select the columns and set the format of the data they contain. Keep the **General** format for the data in the columns 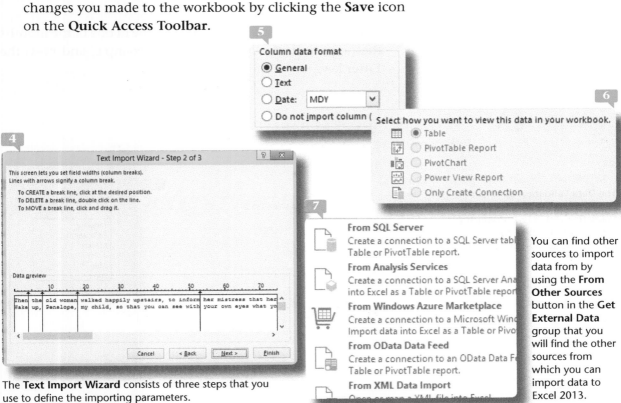 and click the **Finish** button.

8. Text type data can only be imported as a table, 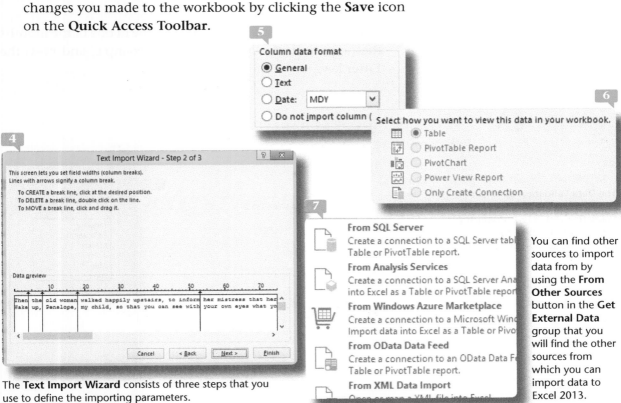 but you can also choose where it will be placed in the present sheet or in a new sheet. Click on the **OK** button on the **Import Data** dialog box so that the text data is imported as a table and placed starting from the selected cell.

9. You are now going to see what other sources you can import data from. Click on a blank cell.

10. Click on the **From Other Sources** tool in the **Get External Data** group.

11. A new feature in Excel 2013 is that you can now import data from more sources such as charts or pivot tables and sources such as OData, Windows Azure DataMarket, and Sharepoints as well as OLE DB suppliers. 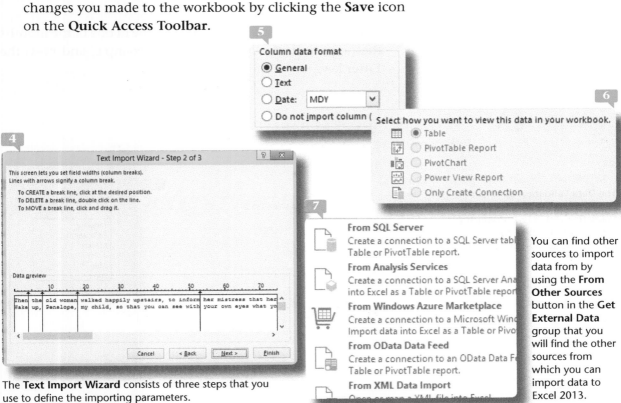 To finish this exercise, save the changes you made to the workbook by clicking the **Save** icon on the **Quick Access Toolbar**.

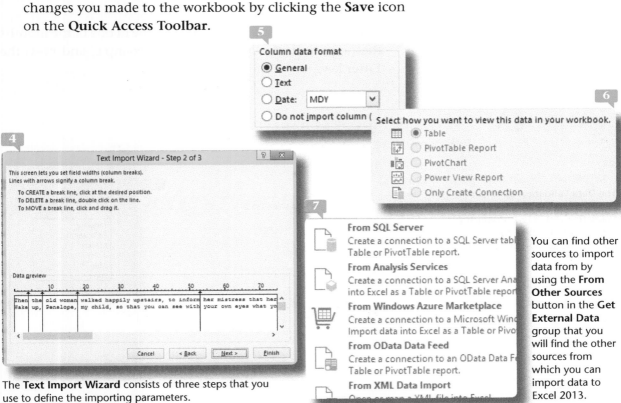

The **Text Import Wizard** consists of three steps that you use to define the importing parameters.

You can find other sources to import data from by using the **From Other Sources** button in the **Get External Data** group that you will find the other sources from which you can import data to Excel 2013.

Validating data

VALIDATING DATA ALLOWS YOU TO RESTRICT the type of data located in a cell, row, or column. You can restrict numeric, text, and formula data.

1. In this exercise you will use Sheet1 from the sample workbook **Autofilter.xlsx**. Click in cell **F2**, click on the **Data** tab on the **Ribbon**, and click on the **Data Validation** command in the **Data Tools** group. 🔲

2. Click on the arrow in the **Data Validation** dialog box to open the **Allow** list and select the **List** option. 🔲

3. Click in the **Source** field, use the **Shift** key to select cell range **A2:A7**, and click on the **OK** button.

4. Notice that next to the selected cell, **F2**, there is an arrow that allows you to open the allowed data drop-down list. Click on it. 🔲

5. Click on cell **F2** again and manually type in one of the months that appear on the list, **January** for example, and press the **Enter** key.

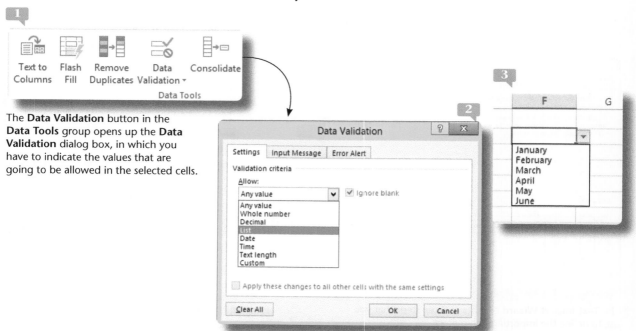

The **Data Validation** button in the **Data Tools** group opens up the **Data Validation** dialog box, in which you have to indicate the values that are going to be allowed in the selected cells.

6. Click on the same cell, type **August** and press the **Enter** key.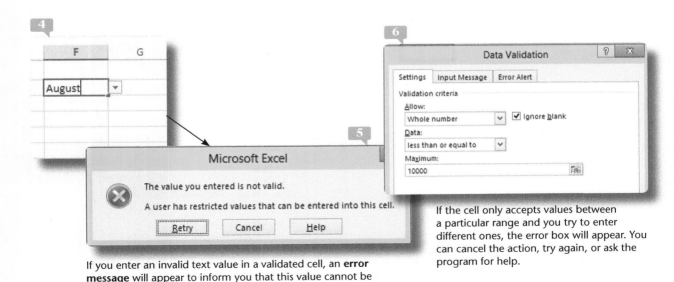

7. A dialog box will open that tells you that the data you entered is not valid. Click on the **Cancel** button in this box.

8. Select cell **G1** and click the **Data Validation** button again.

9. Open the **Allow** list, select **Whole number**, pull down the **Data** list, and select the **less than or equal to** option.

10. Click in the **Maximum** field, type **10000** without any commas, and click on the **OK** button.

11. In cell **G1**, which is already selected, type **10001** and click the **Enter** key.

12. The error alert message appears again as specified in the Data Validation box. Click on the **Retry** button, type **9950**, and click **Enter**.

13. You are now going to see what kind of messages can be found in the **Validation** function. Click on the **Data Validation** button again, and click on the **Error Alert** tab in the dialog box of the same name.

14. In the **Style** field, click the arrow button to see the three message styles and select **Warning**, for example, to see its icon.

15. Finish the exercise by clicking on the **Cancel** button in the **Data Validation** dialog box.

If you enter an invalid text value in a validated cell, an **error message** will appear to inform you that this value cannot be entered in that cell.

If the cell only accepts values between a particular range and you try to enter different ones, the error box will appear. You can cancel the action, try again, or ask the program for help.

Subtotaling data

THE SUBTOTAL FUNCTION, which is located in teh Outline group on the Data tab, allows you to insert subtotals into your table. If you indicate what column contains the data to be calculated and where in the chart the calculation must appear, you can insert partial sums, averages, products, and counts; and you can even calculate maximum and minimum values.

1. For this exercise, you will use the **Points2.xlsx** file again. Open it and click in cell **A1**.

2. Click the **Subtotal** command in the **Outline** group on the **Data** tab. 🔲

3. The **Subtotal** dialog box opens. Keep the default settings and click on the **OK** button. 🔲

4. Just like the dialog box suggested, subtotals have been added. On the left side of the spreadsheet you will now see the usual outline controls. Click on number **1**, which is at the top of the controls, in order to reveal level 1. 🔲

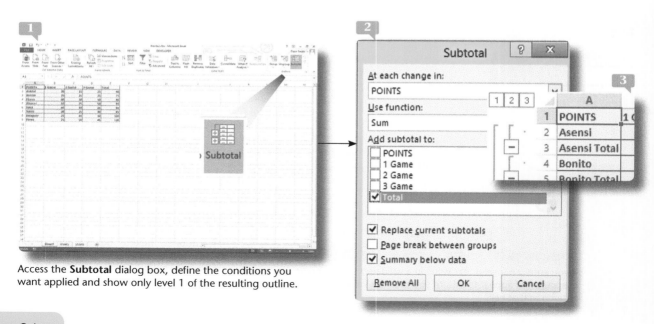

Access the **Subtotal** dialog box, define the conditions you want applied and show only level 1 of the resulting outline.

036

5. In what is called level 1, you are only shown the grand total. Click on number **2** in the control box and see what types of subtotals appear.

6. It is possible to get different view levels. In order to combine the view levels, click on the first +.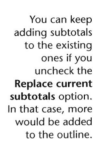

7. The data that corresponds to the first item in your list looks incomplete, that is to say, in level 3. Click the **Subtotal** command again.

8. Pull down the list from the **Use function** drop-down list and select the **Average** option.

9. Uncheck the **Replace current subtotals** option so that the set subtotals do not disappear and click the **OK** button.

10. When you set a new type of subtotal, you add a new level to the outline. Click in level **4** to get a complete view of the table.

11. To finish the exercise, remove all the subtotals. Go to the **Subtotal** dialog box and click the **Remove All** button to return to your original table.

You can keep adding subtotals to the existing ones if you uncheck the **Replace current subtotals** option. In that case, more would be added to the outline.

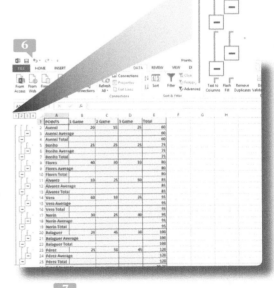

In order to get the different view levels, click on the + and - signs that appear when you create the subtotals outline.

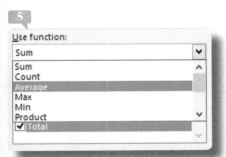

You can use the **Subtotal** box to select among different functions, in order to create an outline (sum, maximum, product, average, etc.).

In order to delete all the subtotals, use the **Remove All** button in the **Subtotal** dialog box.

Editing the contents of a cell

IMPORTANT

Remember the following shortcut: **Ctrl + B** to apply bold, **Ctrl + I** for italics, **Ctrl + U** to underline text.

Underline (Ctrl+U)
Underline your text.

WHEN WE TALK ABOUT EDITING THE CONTENTS of a cell, we mean changing its font, style, color, size, fill color, etc. All those properties can be defined in the Source group on the Home tab, on the Options Ribbon.

1. Imagine you want to apply text and fill cell formats to a particular cell range in your Sheet1. Select rows **1** to **9** for columns **C** and **D** and select the **Home** tab on the **Ribbon**.

2. Keep both columns selected during the exercise. Pull down the list that shows the selected font in the **Font** group and choose one of the fonts that are installed on your computer.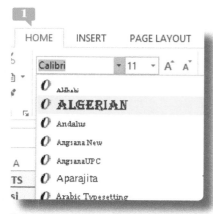

3. You will now change font size. Click the arrow button for the **Font size** pull-down list and choose one of the listed sizes.

4. Notice that the size of the cells starts adjusting according to their contents. The buttons located to the right of the **Font size** field allow you to increase or reduce that size. Click on the **Increase font size** button to see what happens.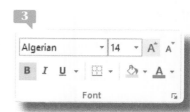

You will find all the necessary tools to edit a cell's contents in the **Font** group, on the **Home** tab. Change the font and its size from there and analyze the effects of the **Increase size** function.

Excel 2013 shows a preview of the selected style before asking you to confirm the choice. You can check it by placing the cursor on any of the fonts or sizes without clicking, and you will notice that the contents of the selected cells change accordingly.

037

5. Apply the **Bold** and **Italics** styles by clicking on the first two icons that appear under the name of the font.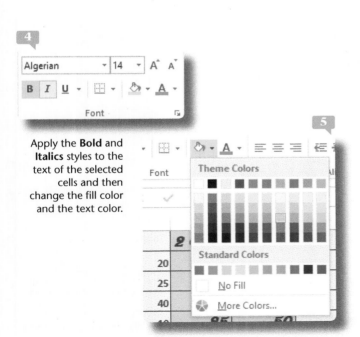

6. You will now change the fill color and the font color. Click on the arrow button for the **Fill Color** icon, which shows a paint bucket, and select one of the colors from the palette in the drop-down list.

7. The selected color is applied to the background of the cell. Click on the arrow button for the **Font Color** icon, which shows an underlined letter **A** and once again select one color from the palette.

8. As you can see, editing the contents of a field is not difficult. Before you finish, go to the **Font** tab in the **Format Cells** dialog box from which you can also see the text characteristics and edit them. Click on the button in the **Font** group to open the dialog box.

9. In this box you can see all the characteristics you have selected for your cell range. Use this box to change the **Italic Bold** type to **Bold** by selecting it in the **Style** box and click **OK** to apply the new style.

10. Finally, deselect the cell range by clicking on any cell to see the result of the changes and save the changes.

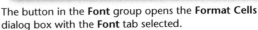

The button in the **Font** group opens the **Format Cells** dialog box with the **Font** tab selected.

Aligning and orienting text in a cell

THE DATA YOU ENTER IN A CELL is aligned left if it contains text or right if it contains numbers. This configuration, which is called General, can be edited by the user. Vertically, data of any kind is always placed at the bottom of the cell.

1. For this exercise, you will keep working with the **Points2.xlsx** workbook. The vertical and horizontal alignment tools can be found in the **Alignment** group on the **Home** tab. Select a text cell and click on the second vertical alignment icons in order to center its contents vertically. **1**

2. Center the contents horizontally as well by clicking on the **Center** icon, which is the second horizontal alignment icons. **2**

3. Click on the **Align Right** command, which is located to the right of the **Center** command. **3**

4. You will change the text orientation for the same cell, and for that you will use the various options included in the **Orien-**

By default, Excel left-aligns text horizontally and bottom-aligns text vertically. Try centering them both ways and then check to see how the **Align Right** tool behaves.

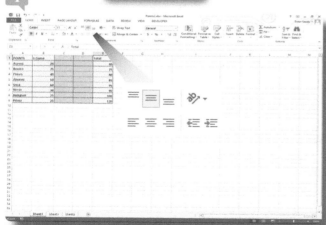

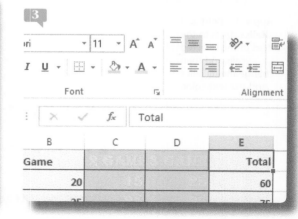

038

tation command. Click on that icon, which is represented by the slanted letters ab.

5. This command lets you apply ascending and descending angles to the text, change its orientation to vertical, rotate it up or down, and access the **Format Cell Alignment** dialog box. Click on the **Angle Counterclockwise** option. 4

6. Click on this command again and this time, select **Vertical Text**. 5

7. Go to the **Format Cell Alignment** dialog box from the **Orientation** tool or by using the button in the **Alignment** group, which opens the dialog box.

8. The **Format Cells** dialog box, which gives you all the format information about the selected text, opens up with the **Alignment** tab selected. To align the text horizontally again, all you have to do is click on the word **Text** that appears on a black background in the **Orientation** section. To tilt the text, type **-45** in the **Degrees** field, 6 click the **OK** button, and look at the result. 7

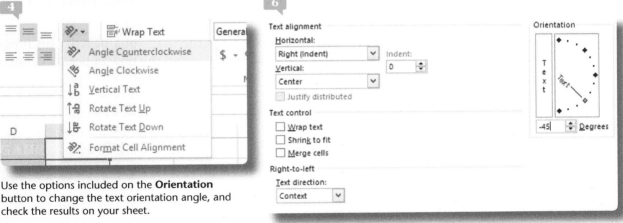

Use the options included on the **Orientation** button to change the text orientation angle, and check the results on your sheet.

You can apply a specific angle by defining it in the **Orientation** field on the **Alignment** tab in the **Format Cells** dialog box, either by typing in the angle value or by dragging the **Text Outline** to the right position.

Adding borders and patterns to a cell

BY DEFAULT, EXCEL KEEPS THE BACKGROUND of the sheets white, the data black, and the gridlines between rows and columns gray. The program allows you to set a number of patterns for the cell backgrounds, which can be combined with the fill colors that you apply to the cells, and it also allows you to insert gridlines.

1. In your sheet, select the range of cells that you want to frame in a box.

2. Click on the arrow next to the **Borders** icon in the **Font** group, next to the **Fill color** tool.

3. You can now see all the default borders that are available in Excel. In this case, select the **Thick Box Border** option.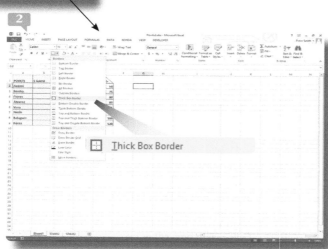

4. The selected range will display a border around it. Click on a cell outside the range to check that.

5. Click on the arrow next to the **Borders** command once more and select the **Draw Border** option.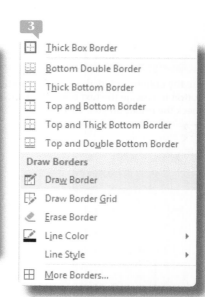

6. Notice that the cursor takes the shape of a pencil. This function allows you to manually assign the type of border defined

The **Border** tool opens up a drop-down menu with all the border options offered by Excel 2013.

039

in the **Borders** command. Click on that command again. Click the **Line Color** option and select a color from the palette.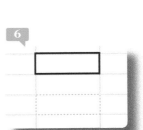

7. You will now choose a border style. Pull down the borders menu again, click on the **Line Style** option, and select one of the dotted lines.

8. Once you have defined the border, click on a blank cell and drag until its four corners are outlined.

9. Deselect the **Draw Border** command by clicking on it.

10. You will now learn how to apply a background pattern to a cell. Go to the **Format Cells** dialog box by selecting that option from the contextual tab on the selected cell and select the **Fill** tab.

11. Click on the arrow in the **Pattern Style** and click on one of the available patterns.

12. The **Sample** box shows you a preview of the selected pattern. Click on the arrow button in the **Pattern Color** field, select a color, and click **OK**.

13. Select another cell to check the result.

14. Select the cells with borders and a pattern again, click on the **Borders** icon in the **Font** group and click the **No Border** option to remove all borders.

6

You can apply the **Draw** tool edge to as many cells as you want.

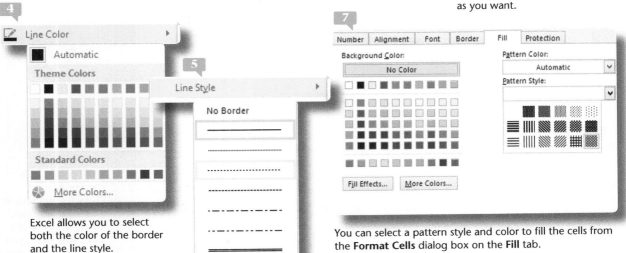

4
Line Color
Automatic
Theme Colors
Standard Colors
More Colors...

Excel allows you to select both the color of the border and the line style.

5
Line Style
No Border

7
Number | Alignment | Font | Border | Fill | Protection
Background Color:
No Color
Pattern Color:
Automatic
Pattern Style:
Fill Effects... | More Colors...

You can select a pattern style and color to fill the cells from the **Format Cells** dialog box on the **Fill** tab.

Applying and creating cell styles

IN ORDER TO APPLY A SPECIFIC CELL format in just one step to one or several cells, you can use cell styles. Excel 2013 offers a large array of cell styles that include format characteristics such as fonts, borders, cell fill, etc. The program allows you to edit a default style in order to create a custom one.

1. Select the cell range to which you want to apply a style.

2. One the **Home** tab in the **Ribbon** click on the **Cell Styles** tool in the **Styles** group.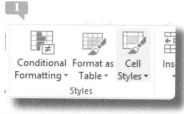

3. This opens a drop-down menu containing the different default styles in Excel. Select the **Accent2** style.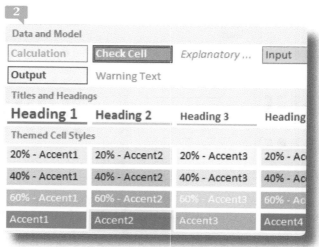

4. If the cells you selected are empty, click on one of them, type a number, and press **Enter** to see what the default text format for the chosen style is. (If the cell was not empty, you would have seen the result directly.)

5. You will now learn how to create a custom cell style. Click on the button for the **Styles** group to open the Styles gallery again and click on the **New Cell Style** option.

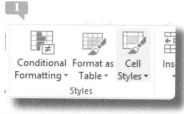

You can find the default styles that are available in Excel 2013 by using the **Cell Styles** button. You can select one of those styles or create your own custom one.

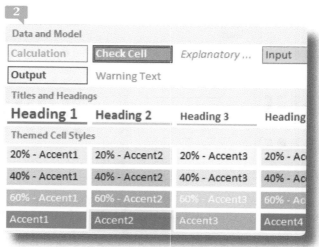

Every default style has a number of characteristics such as a background color, an alignment, and a text color, which you can check by applying it to one of the cells.

6. The **Style** dialog box opens, and the first thing you will do is choose a name. Type a name in the **Style name** field to identify your style. [3]

7. Once you have named your new style, specify what fields you want to define with this style: font, alignment, borders, fill, etc.

8. In order to choose the format you want to apply to the style, click the **Format** button.

9. The **Format Cells** dialog box, which you are already familiar with, appears. You will have to define the characteristics of your cell style in each of the tabs in the box. For example, select light blue in the **Fill** tab. [4]

10. Select the **Border** tab, check the **Outline** option, click on the arrow button in the **Color** field, and select yellow.

11. Ensure that the contents of the cells always left-align. Select the **Alignment** tab and select the **Left (indent)** option in the **Horizontal** field.

12. Click the **OK** button to apply the new format and click that button again in the **Style** box to create the style.

13. In order to apply the newly created style to the selected cell, click on the **Cell Styles** button and, after checking that your style is listed in the **Custom** section, select it. [5]

14. To finish this exercise, select all the columns in the **Points** table and apply the **Output** style to them. (Make sure that all the cells have the same alignment and orientation.)

IMPORTANT

Each of the cell styles has a dialog box that lets you duplicate, delete, or edit the style.

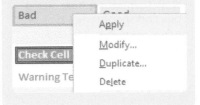

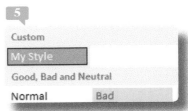

When you create a custom cell style, it will show in the **Custom** section of the gallery.

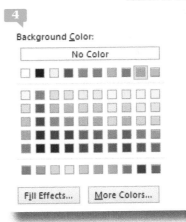

Assign a name to your new style, specify its design and format characteristics, and click on the **Format** button to reach the **Format Cells** dialog box and define the characteristics.

Select a fill color, a border, an alignment, and other characteristics for your custom style from the **Format Cells** dialog box.

Applying conditional formatting

YOU CAN USE CELL CONDITIONAL FORMATTING to visually analyze data on a sheet. The Conditional Formatting command is in the Style group on the Home tab, and it allows you to easily highlight data that you want emphasized when comply specific requirements.

1. In this exercise, you will learn how to apply conditional formatting to cells in a table. You want to highlight the highest scores for 35 of the players in the **Points** table. Select the cell range that contains the scores per game and click on the **Conditional Formatting** command in the **Styles** group. 🔳

2. Conditional formatting allows you to highlight cell rules and top and bottom rules as well as to use data bars, color scales, or icon sets for analysis and presentation. Also, you can create more rules from this Options menu, you can clear the rules you applied, and you can access the **Conditional Formatting Rules Manager**, from which you can edit the rules you created. Select the **Highlight Cell Rules** option. 🔳

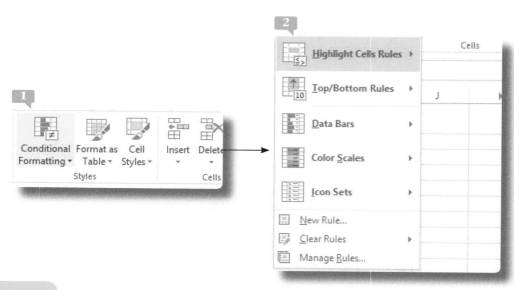

The **Conditional Formatting** command in the **Styles** group, on the **Home** tab, includes several options to highlight cells that meet certain conditions in order to make analysis easier or to improve the appearance of the spreadsheet.

041

3. You can highlight cells that contain values greater or smaller than a certain number, the ones that contain a specific text or date, etc. In this case, click on the **Greater Than** option.

4. The **Greater Than** dialog box opens and this is where you have to specify what value will be used to establish the rule and what the format of the cell abiding by this rule will be. In the **Format cells that are GREATER THAN** input box, type **35**.

5. Notice how, as you enter the values, the cells that abide by the rules get the default formatting, which is **Light Red Fill with Dark Red Text**. Click on the arrow button in the **with** field, click on the **Green Fill with Dark Green Text** option, and click **Enter**.

6. You will now use data bars to show a graphic representation of a value scale in which greater values will display longer bars and smaller ones will display shorter bars. Click on the **Conditional Formatting** button again.

7. Click on the **Data Bars** option and choose the third style in the first row the styles that are available.

8. This graphic representation allows you to quickly see the cells with the highest values. Clear all the conditional formatting that you have applied. Click once again on the **Conditional Formatting** button, click on the **Clear Rules** option and then select the **Clear Rules from Selected Cells** option from the drop-down menu.

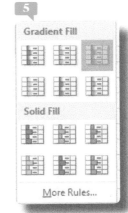

When you select the **Greater Than** option, a dialog box opens in which you have to define the value and the type of fill that will identify the cells that follow the rule.

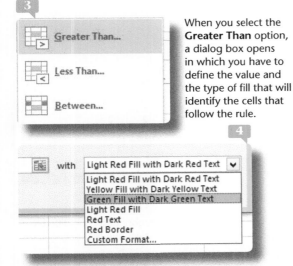

POINTS	1 Game	2 Game	3 Game	Total
Asensi	20	15	25	
Bonito	25	25	25	
Flores	40	30	10	
Álvarez	10	25	50	
Vera	60	10	25	
Nerín	30	25	40	
Balaguer	25	45	30	1

You can also create data bar graphs with different formats.

Number and date formatting

IMPORTANT

In order to display a date in the 01/01/2013 format, select the **Short Date** option from the number format list.

Short Date

WHEN YOU ENTER A NUMERIC VALUE in a cell, it can look very different depending on the formatting that has been assigned to that cell. By default, both text and numeric data use the General format.

1. Select a cell from your table, type **-5** and press **Enter**.

2. Keep the same cell selected while you click on the **Format** button in the **Cells** group and click on the **Format Cells** option. [1]

3. Select the **Number** tab, and after having checked that the present data format is indeed **General**, select the **Number** option. [2]

4. In this format, negative numbers can be expressed in several ways. Select the second option on the **Negative numbers** menu [3] so that negative numbers will show in red and without being preceded by a minus sign (-), and press **Enter**.

5. Numbers are separated by a comma between thousands to make them easier to read. You can pick a format to do that, but you will now learn a simple and fast way to do it. Click on a blank cell, type **2550** and press the **Enter** button.

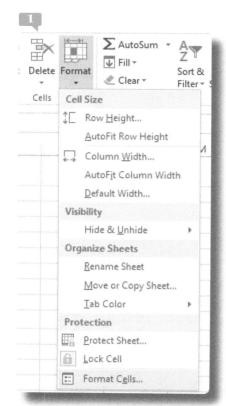

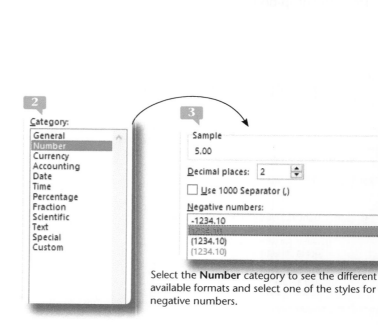

Select the **Number** category to see the different available formats and select one of the styles for negative numbers.

042

6. In the **Number** group, click the **Comma Style** command, which looks like a comma, in order to add the comma that will separate thousands for the numeric value you entered.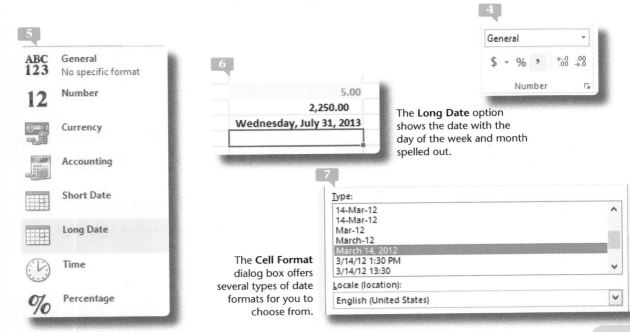

7. You will now apply the date format to cells. Select an empty cell and click on the arrow button in the **Number Format** field located in the **Number** group. There, the default selected option will be **General**.

8. There are two different date styles in this menu. Select the **Long Date** option.

9. Enter the present date (you can separate the fields with forward slashes or with hyphens) and press the **Enter** key.

10. Excel will show you the whole date corresponding to the values you entered. You are now going to use a different way to apply formatting to a date in another cell. Click on the dialog box launcher in the **Number** group.

11. The **Format Cells** dialog box opens again and, this time, you can choose another date format. Click on the **Date** option in the **Category** box.

12. Click on the bottom of the **Type** section scroll bar, select the **March 14, 2012** option, and click the **OK** button.

13. Once the cell format has been selected, all you have to do is type in the current date and press **Enter**.

The **Long Date** option shows the date with the day of the week and month spelled out.

The **Cell Format** dialog box offers several types of date formats for you to choose from.

Calculating elapsed days between dates

IF YOU WANT TO FIND OUT HOW MANY DAYS have elapsed between specific dates, you can use the Today function from the Date & Time category, in the Insert Function dialog box.

1. Select a blank cell from your spreadsheet, select the **Formulas** tab, and click on the **Insert Function** command.

2. In the **Insert Function** dialog box, click on the arrowhead button in the **Or select** a **category** field and select the **Date & Time** option.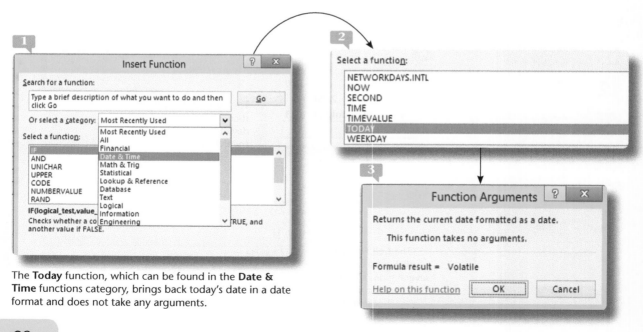

3. All the functions that deal with days, months, years, hours, etc., can be found in this category. Click on the bottom part of the vertical scroll bar in the **Select a function** section, select the **TODAY** option, and click on the **OK** button.

4. The **Function Arguments** dialog box will then open, which shows a brief description of the formula; in this case, it does not take any arguments. You can click on the **Help on this function** link if you want to get more information. Click on the **OK** button for the current date to appear in its cell.

The **Today** function, which can be found in the **Date & Time** functions category, brings back today's date in a date format and does not take any arguments.

5. Notice that Excel automatically applies the date format to the selected cell, so that today's date will be shown in the cell. Click on the **Formula Bar**, at the end of the function, and type a minus sign (-) preceding your date of birth in quotation marks (example: =TODAY()-"10/09/1984").

6. It is very important to enter the date enclosed in quotation marks so that the action is performed correctly. Click the **Enter** button.

7. Since the selected cell format is a date format, Excel offers you the result of the function in that same format. You are going to change it in order to see the number of days that have elapsed since your day of birth. Keep the cell selected and select the **Home** tab again, click on the arrowhead button in the **Number Format** field, and select the **Number** option.

8. In order to check that the result is correct, you will do the simple division in another cell. Select a blank cell and type the following formula: **=name of the cell that contains the result to function TODAY/365** (number of days in the year).

9. Click the **Enter** button on the **Formula Bar** and check that the result corresponds to your exact age expressed in years.

10. To finish the exercise, click on the **Save** icon in the **Quick Access Toolbar** to save the changes.

4

| f_x | =TODAY()-"10/09/1984" |

Remember to type the date in quotes for the formula to work correctly.

5

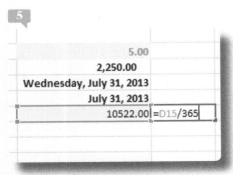

	5.00
	2,250.00
Wednesday, July 31, 2013	
	July 31, 2013
10522.00	=D15/365

The **Today** formula changes the cell to the date format. Change that format to **Number**.

6

	5.00	
	2,250.00	
Wednesday, July 31, 2013		
	July 31, 2013	
10522.00	28.8273973	

In order to get the result in years, select the other empty cell and enter the formula: **=name of the cell that contains the result to function TODAY/365**.

Experimenting with other formats

THERE IS A VAST NUMBER OF FORMAT CATEGORIES for numeric values: currency, percentage, time, fraction, etc. In this exercise, you will practice with some of those formats. You will make the changes through the Cell format dialog box, and you will also use the list of formats that can be found in the Number group, on the Home tab.

1. Select a range of cells with numeric values and the **General** format from your spreadsheet.

2. Click on the arrowhead button in the **Number Format** field in the **Number** group, on the **Home** tab. [1]

3. A list with the main available number format types will appear. Click on the **Percentage** option. [2]

4. The values of the selected range cells are now shown in percentages with two decimals, [3] according to the **Format Cells** box default settings. You can use the two icons on the dialog box launcher, in the **Number** group, to increase or decrease the number of decimals. In order to decrease the number of decimals in the selected cells, click on the **Decrease Decimal** tool, which is the second icon. [4]

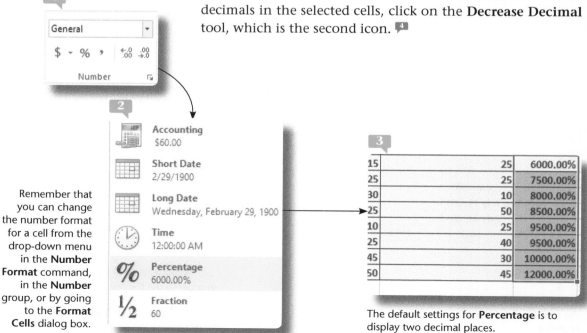

Remember that you can change the number format for a cell from the drop-down menu in the **Number Format** command, in the **Number** group, or by going to the **Format Cells** dialog box.

Accounting	$60.00	
Short Date	2/29/1900	
Long Date	Wednesday, February 29, 1900	
Time	12:00:00 AM	
Percentage	6000.00%	
Fraction	60	

15	25	6000.00%
25	25	7500.00%
30	10	8000.00%
25	50	8500.00%
10	25	9500.00%
25	40	9500.00%
45	30	10000.00%
50	45	12000.00%

The default settings for **Percentage** is to display two decimal places.

5. Notice that the selected values only show one decimal now. You can also change the number of decimals and the format number from the **Format Cells** dialog box. Click on the dialog box launcher in the **Number** group and try changing the number of decimals.

6. You will now see how many time formats are available in Excel. Click on the **Time** category and select the third type of format from the **Type** section.

7. If there were no times in the selected cells, Excel will, by default, show midnight in the desired format. Click the **OK** button. **5**

8. You will now apply the **number with zero decimal places** style to the selected cells. Click on the arrowhead button in the **Number** format field that now shows the **Time** option, and click on the **More Number Formats** command.

9. The **Format Cells** dialog box opens again with the **Number** tab selected. Click on the **Number** category.

10. Type **0** in the **Decimal** places box or use the side arrows to lower the number to zero, **6** and click the **OK** button.

11. To finish this exercise, deselect the cell range by clicking on an empty cell and use the **Ctrl + S** shortcut to save the changes.

044

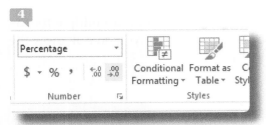

The **Increase Decimal** and the **Decrease Decimal** commands allow you to easily edit the number of decimals that will show in a cell with a numeric value.

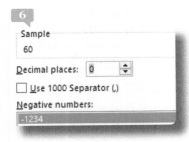

You can edit the number of decimals from the **Format Cells** dialog box by changing the number of decimal places from the **Number** category.

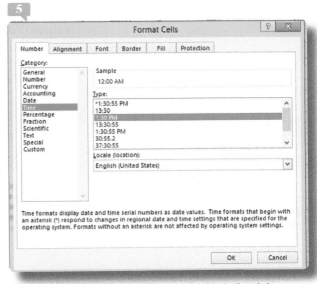

See what the different time formats available in Excel do.

Using the AutoComplete function

WHEN YOU ENTER A FUNCTION, Excel 2013 selects the Auto-Complete function, by default, with which you can quickly type a formula. This function, which can be selected or deselected from the Formulas tab in the Excel Options dialog box, detects the functions that you want to use and offers help to complete the correct formula.

1. To begin this exercise, which will teach you how to use the **AutoComplete** function, click on the **File** tab, and click on the **Options** command.

2. In the **Excel Options** dialog box, click on the **Formulas** option in the left pane.

3. Make sure that the **Formula AutoComplete** option in the **Working with formulas** section is selected. ▛ That is why, when you start entering a formula, a list of functions whose first letter matches the first letter you entered, appears. Click on the **Cancel** button to close the **Excel Options** dialog box.

4. To start entering a function, select a blank cell on your sheet and type =. ▟

5. Imagine you want to find the least common multiple for the values of three cells from this sheet, but you do not know the syntax for this function. Enter **L**.

You can select or deselect the **AutoComplete** function from the **Formula** tab in the **Excel Options** dialog box or you can press the **Alt + down arrow** shortcut in the formula edit mode to make the list of functions disappear.

1

Working with formulas

☐ R1C1 reference style ⓘ
☑ Formula AutoComplete ⓘ
☑ Use table names in formulas
☑ Use GetPivotData functions for PivotTable references

Error Checking

☑ Enable background error checking

2

Wednesday, July 31, 2013	
July 31, 2013	
10522.00	28.8273973
=	

Remember that in Excel, a formula must always be preceded by =.

045

6. The **AutoComplete** list appears, and you can see all the functions whose first letter matches the letter you entered. When you select the functions on this list, the program shows you a brief description of how to enter the correct information for the function. Click on the **LCM.** (**least common multiple**) function.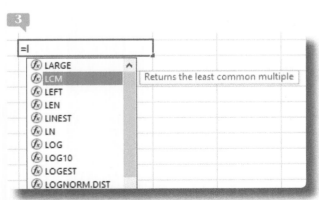

7. Double-click on this function in order to select it and insert it.

8. A tag will appear with the correct function syntax, containing all the numbers for which you want to find the least common multiple. Select the cell that will act as the first variable by clicking on it.

9. As indicated in the ScreenTip, the variables have to be separated by a colon and enclosed in parentheses. **Enter** a comma and select the cell that will serve as the second variable.

10. Enter another colon and select a third cell.

11. You already know that when you enter a function you must not forget to close the parentheses, the square bracket for a reference chart, or the quotation marks for an **MDX** text connection string. Insert a right parenthesis and press **Enter** to confirm entering the function.

12. Click on the **Save** icon, on the **Quick Access Toolbar** to save the changes.

IMPORTANT

The **AutoComplete** function helps you to enter a formula or a function's data and signs, and guides you to ensure a correct result.

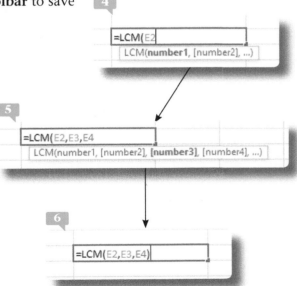

After typing = and the first letter, or a display trigger, Excel shows a drop-down list of valid functions, names, and text connection strings that match the letters or the trigger.

You will notice that when you close the parentheses and complete the function, as indicated on the **AutoComplete** tag, the help disappears, which confirms that the format of the function is correct. If it were not correct, the tag would not disappear.

Analyzing data instantly

Excel 2013 offers a new instant data analysis tool that lets you convert your data into a chart or table in a few steps and also lets you preview your data with conditional formatting, sparklines, or charts.

1. The new **Quick Analysis** tool appears when you select a range of cells with data. Use **Sheet1** of the **Points2.xlsx** workbook that you have been practicing with in the last few exercises. Select cell range **E2:E9**, which are where the total scores are.

2. The **Quick Analysis** tool icon appears in the lower left corner of the selected range. Click on it. ⬛

3. The Quick Analysis palette appears with several tabs that you can use depending on the result you want (changing the format, getting charts, calculating totals, and creating tables or sparklines). The first tab is called **Formatting**, which allows you to highlight important data in a range by applying conditional formatting to the cells that abide by certain rules. (Review the exercise on conditional formatting.) Place the cursor on the **Color Scale** option in this tab and see what happens to the selected cells. ⬛

Press the **Ctrl +Q** shortcut to show and hide the **Quick Analysis** icon.

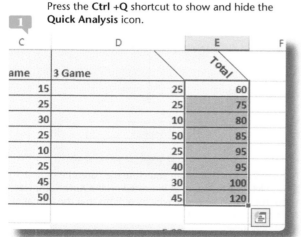

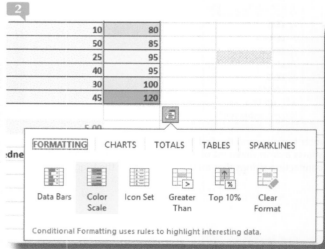

4. With this option, Excel uses different colors to tell greater and lower values apart. Place the cursor on the **Greater Than** option, and after having checked that some specific values are highlighted in red, click to configure the rule. [3]

5. The **Greater Than** dialog box opens, which is where you have to assign a format to the cells that contain a value that is higher than the one you indicated. Double-click on the cell that shows the numeric value and type **80**.

6. You can check the results directly in the selected range. Use the drop-down format option list in the same dialog box and select the **Green Fill with Dark Green Text** option. [4]

7. Click the **OK** button to accept the rule.

8. The new Quick Analysis function allows you to easily and quickly identify data by applying conditional formatting, and to convert that data into graphic representations in only a few steps. If you want to select that function, you have to go to the **General** category in the **Excel Options** dialog box and uncheck the **Show Quick Analysis options on selection** checkbox. [5] To finish this exercise, deselect the range of cells that you have analyzed [6] and save the changes you have made to the sheet.

046

IMPORTANT

You have to remember that the options that appear on the different tabs of the **Quick Analysis** palette can vary depending on the type of data contained in the selected range.

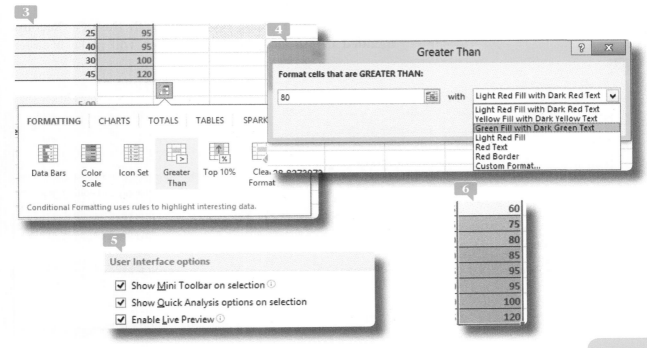

Creating charts

WITH EXCEL 2013'S IMPROVED GRAPHIC TOOLS, creating attractive, professional looking charts is now much faster and easier than it was in earlier versions. The Charts group, from which you can get a preview of all the available chart styles, can be found on the Insert tab, which is on the Ribbon. The dialog box launcher in this section gives you access to the Insert Chart dialog box in which the different styles also appear, sorted into categories.

1. In this first exercise dedicated to charts, you will learn how to create one from a data table. You will keep on working with the **Points2.xlsx** workbook. You have to select a cell range containing the data you are going to represent on the chart. Click on cell **A1**, press on the **Shift** key, and hold it down while you click on cell **E9**.

2. Click on the **Insert** tab, on the **Ribbon**.

3. A new feature in Excel 2013 is **Recommended Charts**, available in the **Charts** group, that recommends the most suitable chart styles for the type of data that you want to represent. Click on that button.

4. The **Insert Chart** dialog box opens with the new **Recommended Charts** tab selected, which will make it easier

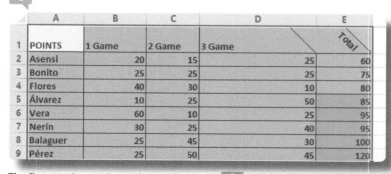

	A	B	C	D	E
1	POINTS	1 Game	2 Game	3 Game	Total
2	Asensi	20	15	25	60
3	Bonito	25	25	25	75
4	Flores	40	30	10	80
5	Álvarez	10	25	50	85
6	Vera	60	10	25	95
7	Nerín	30	25	40	95
8	Balaguer	25	45	30	100
9	Pérez	25	50	45	120

The first step in creating a chart is to select the cell range that contains the information you want to convey.

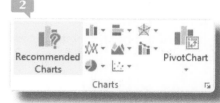

The tools for creating and editing graphics have improved considerably in Excel 2013.

Insert Chart

Recommended Charts | All Charts

Clustered Column - Line

for you to select the best chart type for your data. Select the second recommended chart style, **Clustered Column**, and click the **OK** button.

5. The chart will appear in the middle of the sheet. The data represented on the chart is outlined in blue in the original table. The **Chart Tools** contextual tab in this version of Excel has been simplified to contain only two subtabs: **Design** and **Format**. You will change the chart style in order to make it more attractive. Go to the **Design** subtab and click on the **More** command, which is the third arrow button in the **Chart Styles** group.

6. Click on one of the styles with a dark background in the Chart Styles gallery to apply it.

7. You will now apply one of the chart layouts, the one that allows you to show the total values on the corresponding chart bars. Click on the **Quick Layout** command and then click on the first design in the last row of the Design gallery that has appeared.

8. Deselect the chart and save the changes.

As you have seen for yourself, using a chart to represent numeric data from a table is a pleasant and intelligible way to visualize a dataset that could otherwise seem dense or boring.

047

In earlier versions of Excel, the **Chart Tools** contextual tab was composed of three subtabs. In Excel 2013, this number was reduced to two to make it easier to find what you are looking for.

If none of the recommended charts seems to fit your needs, go to the **All Charts** tab in the **Insert Chart** dialog box and look for another type of chart.

Select a type of chart, a quick style, and a quick design among the many available in the Excel 2013 gallery.

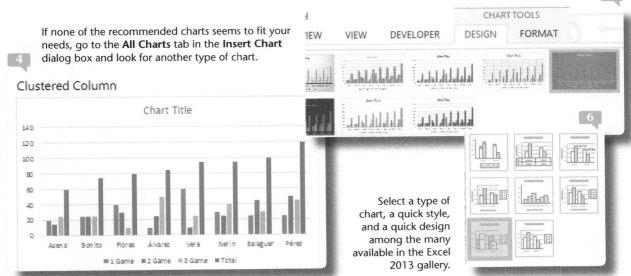

Clustered Column

Modifying a chart

CHART EDITING TOOLS HAVE IMPROVED a lot in Excel 2013 giving way to a more professional look and a faster and easier design. As you saw in the last exercise, when you select a chart, the Chart Tools tab is added on the Ribbon and you can use its Design and Format tabs to modify the aspect of all the elements in the chart, from its legends to its background.

1. In this exercise, you will practice with some of the chart editing tools. In the previous exercise, you used the new **Recommended Charts** function to create your chart and then applied a design and a quick style to it; this time you will start by editing the legend. Click on the chart to select it.

2. When working with charts, another new feature in Excel 2013 is the chart elements controls that appear to its right and that allow you to add, remove, or change elements; set a style; and filter which data will be visible. In order to reposition the legend, click on the Control button, the one with the + , click on the arrowhead button in the **Legend** option from the list of elements that is displayed, and select the **Left** option. 💬**1**

3. You will now apply a background fill to the legend. Click on the arrowhead button in the **Legend** option and this time, select **More Options**. 💬**2**

This menu allows you to reposition the legend, which is placed to the right of the chart area by default.

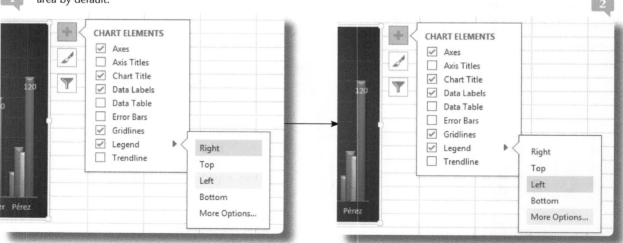

048

4. The legend gets selected on the chart, and it is now ready to be edited from the **Format Legend** pane that is displayed on the right of the work area. Click on the first icon in this pane, which corresponds to the **Fill & Line** tool, and select the drop-down menu in the **Fill** option.

5. This command allows you to apply a solid background color or picture, a gradient fill, or a texture fill. Select the **Solid fill** option,  click on the color sample, and select the one you prefer as a background for the legend.

6. In order to apply an effect to the selected element, (shadow, glow, reflection), click on the second icon, **Effects**, display the **Glow** effects, and select a default one from the **Glow Varia-tions** group.

7. You can keep on editing the fill, outline, and text position of the legend if you select the **Text Options** section on the **Legend** format panel. Click on the X button on the header to close that panel.

8. Click on any blank cell to deselect the chart and see the results more clearly, 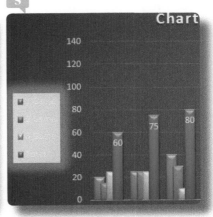 and click on the **Save** icon on the **Quick Access Toolbar** to save the changes you made to the sheet.

You can also use the **Add Chart Element** tool on the **Design** subtab, located on the **Chart Tools** contextual tab, to reposition a chart legend.

Remember that you can edit the legend from the **Ribbon** if you check this element in the **Current Selection** group, on the **Format** subtab located on the **Chart Tools** contextual tab.

You can apply all kinds of effects with Excel (shadow, glow, beveled edges, or reflection) to almost any element of a chart.

Changing chart backgrounds and titles

EXCEL 2013 CHART TOOLS INCLUDE SPECIAL effects such as 3D, transparency, and soft shadows. The different elements that make up a chart (chart area, legend, title, labels, plot area) can be edited both from the Chart Tools contextual tabs and by using the new controls that appear when you select them. You can add a background to the chart; reposition it; edit the style of the title, the legend, or the labels; and move the chart, among many other actions.

1. In this exercise you will add a custom background to the chart and change its title. Select the chart.

2. Right-click on the chart background and select the **Format Chart Area** option from the drop-down menu.

3. The **Format Chart Area** box opens from which you can edit the fill and lines of the chart area and apply shadows and 3D effects to it. In this case, you will apply a background texture. In the **Fill** section, select the **Picture or texture fill** radio button. 2

4. You can apply a preset texture, which you have stored in your system, or one of the predesigned pictures. Click on the **Texture** field button. 3

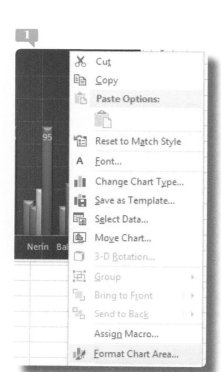

2
▲ FILL

○ No fill
○ Solid fill
○ Gradient fill
◉ Picture or texture fill
○ Pattern fill

You can edit the width of the **Format** pane by dragging its left margin.

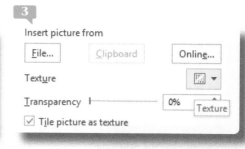

3
Insert picture from

| File... | Clipboard | Online... |

Texture

Transparency |———————— | 0% | Texture

☑ Tile picture as texture

You can apply a solid fill, a gradient fill, or a picture or texture fill to your chart background. Select the **Picture or texture fill** and see what the available textures are.

5. Click on one of the texture options  to select it and check the results on the chart.

6. You will now edit the chart title style. Click directly on that element to select it and see how the format panel adapts to the selection and shows the chart title options.

7. You will edit the title from the **Format** subtab on the **Chart Tools** contextual tab. Select that subtab to display the **WordArt** styles drop-down gallery, and select one of the default styles. **5**

8. Check the effect this had on the chart title. You will now apply a text effect to the title, and this time you will use the format panel. Select the **Text Options** section, click on the second icon that corresponds to the **Text Effects** function, and select the available reflection styles. **6**

9. Select the **Reflection Variations** gallery and select your favorite variation. **7**

10. To finish the exercise, click on the X button to close the **Format Chart Title** panel, click on any cell to deselect the chart, and save the changes.

049

IMPORTANT

The element you selected is checked in the **Current Selection** group. If you make any format or style changes, the changes will be applied to the selected area.

Select a predetermined texture to apply to your chart background, and if you wish, you can edit some of the tile options or its degree of transparency, on the **Chart Area Format** pane.

Pink tissue paper

You can apply a quick style of **WordArt** text to any element of your chart (the title, the legend, the data, etc.).

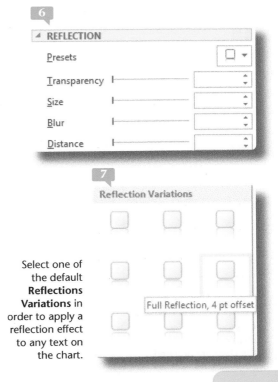

Select one of the default **Reflections Variations** in order to apply a reflection effect to any text on the chart.

Full Reflection, 4 pt offset

Formatting chart data

EVERY DATA POINT IN A CHART can be formatted separately or together with the whole series of points that it is related to. If you click once on a data point, the whole series gets selected. If you click once more, only that data point gets selected. In order to edit the point, you have to use the Format data point or Format series panes, depending on the selected element.

1. Click on one of the columns on your chart and check that the series you are referring to is selected on the spreadsheet.

2. Click on the selection again so that only that portion will be selected on the chart.

3. Select the **Format** subtab on the **Chart Tools** contextual tab and notice that the information about the selected element is displayed in the **Current Selection** group.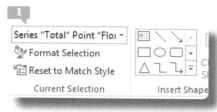

4. On your data table, double-click on the data corresponding to the selected element, 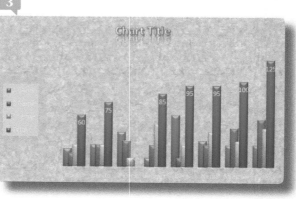 edit its value, and press the **Enter** key to apply the change to your chart.

5. Select the data series you just edited, go to the **Format** subtab and click on the **Format Selection** button in the **Current Selection** group.

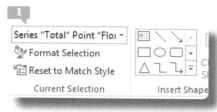

1 Game	2 Game	3 Game
20	15	
25	25	
40	30	
10	25	
60	10	
30	25	
25	45	
25	50	

Change some of the values in your original chart and you will see how the data and the chart are updated.

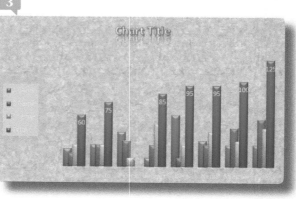

Select the whole series on your chart and then only one of the parts.

6. The **Format Data Series** panel opens and you can use it to modify the series' fill color, border style, etc. In order to decrease the width of the gap between elements, click on the left of the slider control in the **Gap Width** section until it reaches 45%. **4**

7. You will now apply a metallic 3D effect to the portions. Click on the second icon in the panel to select the **Effects** section, and display the **3-D Format** options.

8. As you can see, Excel applies a soft upper bevel effect to the data series by default. Keep this effect and click on the **Material** button. **5**

9. Click to select the last material in the **Standard** section. **6**

10. The editing of charts' data labels has also improved in Excel 2013. Click the button with the + located next to the selected chart, click on the arrowhead in the **Data Labels** element, and select **More Options**.

11. This will launch the **Format Data Labels** panel, from which you can now change the format of those elements while keeping them in place, even if you change the chart type. You can also connect the labels to their data points with leader lines and include updatable rich text format. As an example, select **Inside End** from the **Label Position** section. **7**

12. Close the **Format Data Labels** pane, deselect the chart, and save the changes to finish this exercise.

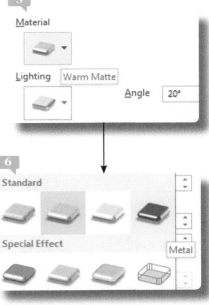

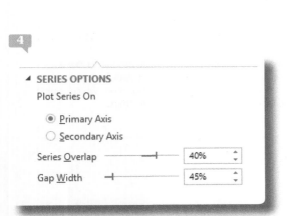

You can edit the fill, the color, and the style of the data series outline from the **Format Data Series** panel, and you can also apply shadow and 3D effects to them.

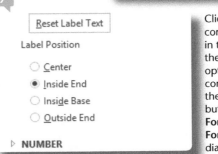

Click on the corresponding button in the Options Ribbon, the corresponding option in its contextual menu, or the new quick edit buttons to open the **Format Series** or **Format Data Point** dialog boxes.

Adding and replacing data in a chart

THERE ARE SEVERAL WAYS YOU CAN ADD data to an Excel chart. You can select the series you want to add, clicking on the copy button on the Home tab, and selecting the Paste option after having selected the chart. Another way you can add data is by using the Select data function on the Chart Tools design tab or on the new Chart Filters button. You can also select an empty range of cells that you want to add to the chart and start adding the values to the spreadsheet one by one; you will notice how the chart updates itself as you enter the values.

1. In this exercise you will learn how to add new data to a chart and replace the existing data. Use the **Points3.xlsx** file, which has been updated with an extra line that you will also be adding to the chart. Select it and click on the new **Chart Filters** button, which looks like a funnel.

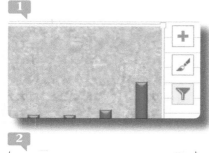

2. Imagine that you added a data row to your source table, and you now want to include it in the chart. Click on the **Select Data** link in the box that has appeared.

3. You can use the **Select Data Source** dialog box to add new data to the chart and also to add, edit, and remove legend entries. Keep this dialog box open and use the **Shift** key to select the A1:E10 cell range.

Select Data Source

Chart data range: =Sheet1!$A$1:$E$9

Switch Row/Column

Legend Entries (Series)
- Add Edit Remove ▲ ▼
- ☑ 1 Game
- ☑ 2 Game
- ☑ 3 Game
- ☑ Total

Horizontal (Category) Axis Labels
- Edit
- ☑ Asensi
- ☑ Bonito
- ☑ Flores
- ☑ Álvarez
- ☑ Vera

Hidden and Empty Cells   OK   Cancel

You can also access this dialog box by using the **Select Data** button on the **Design** subtab of the **Chart Tools** contextual tab.

If you need to temporarily minimize the **Select Data Source** dialog box in order to select data from the source table, click on the Collapse dialog box icon, which is next to the **Chart data range** field in the chart.

	A	B	C	D	E
1	POINTS	1 Game	2 Game	3 Game	Total
2	Asensi	20	15	25	60
3	Bonito	25	25	25	75
4	Flores	40	30	10	80
5	Álvarez	10	25	50	85
6	Vera	60	10	25	95
7	Nerín	30	25	40	95
8	Balaguer	25	45	30	100
9	Pérez	25	55	45	125
10	Smith	30	25	55	110

051

4. In order for the chart to get updated and show the new line of data you have added to the table, click the **OK** button.

5. You can now see that the chart has a new entry, which corresponds to the new entry in the table. Click on the **Chart Filter** icon again and follow the **Select Data** link.

6. Select the **B1:B10** cell range and click on the **Edit** button in the **Horizontal (Category) Axis Labels** section. 5

7. You must now select the cell range that contains the data you want to show in the labels. Click on cell **B2**, press and hold down the **Shift** key, and click on cell **B10**. 6

8. Click on the **OK** button in the **Axis Labels** dialog box and click **OK** again in the **Select Data Source** dialog box.

9. Notice that the chart has been successfully updated. 7 You are now going to see how the program reacts when you delete some data in the source table. Click on cell **B5** to select it and press on the **Delete** key to clear its contents.

10. The chart is automatically updated to match the source information. You will now undo the last few actions in order to change the data back to the way it was before you started this exercise. Click twice on the **Undo** button, on the **Quick Access Toolbar**.

11. Click on the **Save** icon on the **Quick Access Toolbar**.

5

Horizontal (Category) Axis Labels
✎ Edit
☑ Asensi
☑ Bonito
☑ Flores
☑ Álvarez
☑ Vera

6

	A	B	C	D
1	POINTS	1 Game	2 Game	3 Game
2	Asensi	20	15	
3	Bonito	25	25	
4	Flores	40	30	
5	Álvarez	10	25	
6	Vera	60	10	
7	Nerín	30	25	
8	Balaguer	25	45	
9	Pérez	25	55	
10	Smith	30	25	

Remember that in order to select a cell range, you have to click on the first cell and then on the last one while holding the **Shift** key down.

If you modify cell values that are reflected in a chart, the latter will be automatically updated.

7

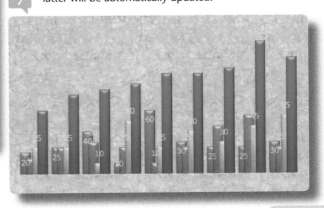

Saving a chart as a template

IF YOU CUSTOMIZED A CHART to meet your needs or your company's and you wish to use this type of chart in further documents, you can store it as a chart template (.crtx format) in the chart template folder, on your computer. When you stop needing it, you can delete it from that folder.

1. In this exercise, you will learn how to save a custom type of chart as a template, retrieve it, and delete it from the chart template folder. Click on the chart to select it.

2. Right-click on the chart and click on the **Save as Template** option from the contextual drop-down menu.

3. The **Save Chart Template** dialog box opens and shows the default path for saving this type of document. Type the name of your template in the **File name** field and click on the **Save** button.

4. The template is now saved in the corresponding Microsoft folder. You will now learn how to retrieve this template in order to apply it to a new chart. Open a new Excel workbook that contains a data table (for example the **AutoFilters** file that you already used previously).

052

5. Select the range of cells that you want to represent on the chart and go to the **Insert** tab.

6. Click on the **Recommended Charts** button in the **Charts** group 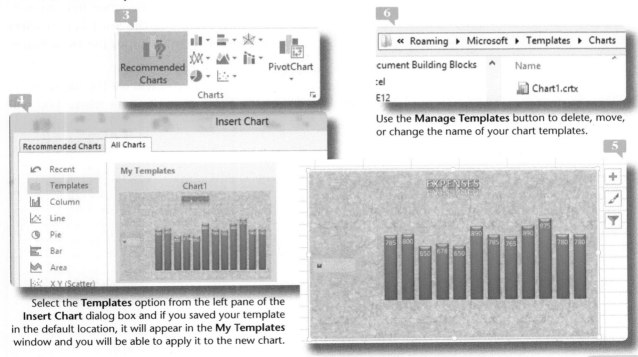 and select the **All Charts** tab from the **Insert Chart** dialog box.

7. Remember that you can also access the **Insert Chart** dialog box by clicking on the **Charts** group dialog box launcher. Select **Templates** from the **Categories** pane on the left.

8. If you have stored your chart template on a default Excel path, it should appear in the box. (If you have saved it in another folder, use the **Manage Templates** button to locate it and move it to the **Charts** folder.) Select your template and click the **OK** button.

9. Notice that the chart you had customized in previous exercises appears now, and use the **Save** command on the **Quick Access Toolbar** to save the changes.

The **Manage Templates** button opens the folder that holds the templates by default. When you stop needing the template, select it and press the **Delete** key to delete it. Also, if you want to copy it to another folder, select it, cut it or copy it, and paste it to the destination of your choice.

Use the **Manage Templates** button to delete, move, or change the name of your chart templates.

Select the **Templates** option from the left pane of the **Insert Chart** dialog box and if you saved your template in the default location, it will appear in the **My Templates** window and you will be able to apply it to the new chart.

Creating sparklines

EXCEL 2013 FEATURES THE SPARKLINE COMMAND, which allows you to create small charts, embedded in a spreadsheet cell. Sparklines help you detect patterns in the data you entered, as they offer a visual representation of the data. You can also type text in the cell where the sparkline is inserted.

1. In this exercise, you will see how to insert sparklines in an Excel sheet. You will keep on using the **Points3.xlsx** sample file. Click on a blank cell, for example **F2**, to select it as a destination for the sparkline.

2. Select the **Insert** tab on the **Ribbon**.

3. Excel allows you to add three types of sparklines: line, column, or win/loss. In this case, you will create a line sparkline. Click on the **Line** option in the **Sparklines** group. 💬

4. The **Create Sparklines** dialog box opens and you have to indicate the range of cells that you want to graph. Your aim is to show a player's progress throughout the three games. Remember that you can, if needed, click on the icons next to each field to collapse the dialog box. Hold the **Shift** key to select the **B2:D2** cell range in order to enter it into the **Data Range** text box. 💬

5. In the **Location Range** text box, you will see the name of the cell you selected at the beginning, the one where you will

	A	B	C	D
1	POINTS	1 Game	2 Game	3 Game
2	Asensi	20	15	25
3	Bonito	25	25	25
4	Flores	40	30	10
5	Alvarez	10	25	50
6	Vera	60	10	25
7	Nerín	30	25	40
8	Balaguer	25	45	30
9	Pérez	25	55	45
10	Smith	30	25	55

053

place the sparklines. 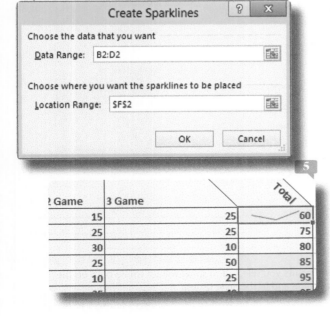 Click on the **OK** button to create the sparklines.

6. The sparklines are inserted. The **Sparkline Tools** contextual tab appears, and the **Design** subtab allows you to edit the appearance of the sparklines. You will try to move the sparkline to a different cell that contains data. Select the cell that contains the sparkline and click on the **Edit Data** button in the **Sparkline** group.

7. Select the **Edit Group Location & Data** option.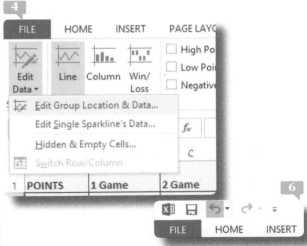

8. The **Edit Sparklines** dialog box opens with the **Location Range** box selected. Click on the cell that corresponds to the total value of the player you chose to be represented on the sparklines.

9. The contents of the **Location Range** box have changed and now show the new location of the sparkline. Click on the **OK** button to see the result.

10. Click on the cell that now contains the sparkline in order to verify that its presence does not prevent you from using the cell normally.

11. Use the **Undo** command on the **Quick Access Toolbar** to return the sparkline to its previous location.

You can apply color combinations from built-in formats to sparklines. When you select the cell that contains the sparkline, the **Chart Tools** contextual tab appears, and you can find all the commands you need on its **Design** subtab to edit this element.

Customizing sparklines

AFTER CREATING SPARKLINES you can manage what value points you show (such as high points, low points, first point, last point, or any negative points), you can change the type of sparkline (line, column, or win/loss), you can apply styles from a gallery, or set individual format options.

1. You will now practice with the different types of sparklines available in Excel 2013. The **Type** group allows you to change the sparkline type after the sparkline has been created. Select the cell in which you inserted the sparkline during the previous exercise, and click on the **Column** button in the **Type** group, on the **Sparkline Tools** tab. 🔲

2. You will notice that the sparkline has been modified. Click on the **Win/Loss** button to see what it looks like and select **Line** again to keep the initial format.

3. You will now request that the highest and lowest scores show on the chart. Go to the **Show** group and check the **High Point** and **Low Point** check boxes. 🔲

4. The changes can be seen on the sparkline. 🔲 You will now apply one of the preset styles available in Excel to the sparkline.

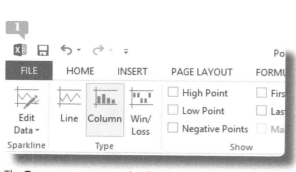

The **Type** group commands offer three options to modify the sparkline type: **Line**, **Column**, and **Win/Loss**.

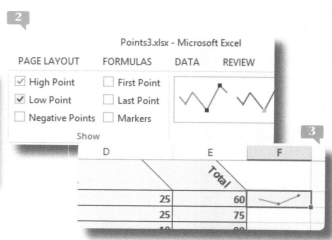

The points you selected to show will be visible both on the sparkline and in the Style group.

In order to do that, click on the **More command** in the Quick Styles pane, in the **Style** group, while keeping the cell that contains the sparkline selected. 🔲

054

5. Select the style you prefer from the drop-down menu.

6. Notice that the style of the sparkline has changed. 🔲 You can also apply custom changes. Keep the sparkline cell selected and click on the **Sparkline Color** button. 🔲

7. Click to select one of the colors from the drop-down palette and notice how it is automatically applied to the sparkline.

8. You can also edit the colors of the high points, low points, etc. Click on the **Marker Color** button and select the **High point** option.

9. Click on the color you want in order to select it.

10. Click on the **Clear** button in the **Group** tool group to delete the sparkline. 🔲

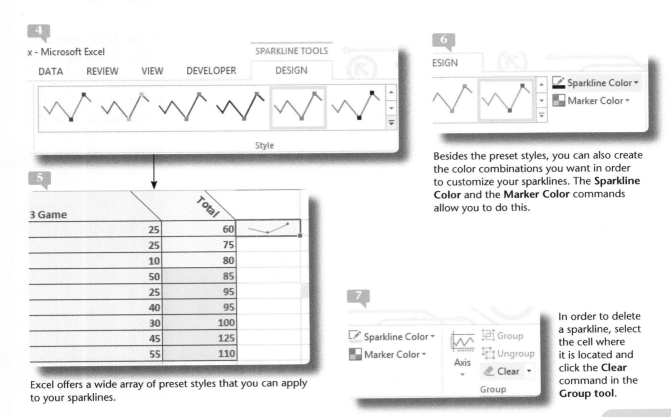

Besides the preset styles, you can also create the color combinations you want in order to customize your sparklines. The **Sparkline Color** and the **Marker Color** commands allow you to do this.

Excel offers a wide array of preset styles that you can apply to your sparklines.

In order to delete a sparkline, select the cell where it is located and click the **Clear** command in the **Group tool**.

Creating and editing SmartArt graphics

DIAGRAMS ALLOW THE GRAPHIC REPRESENTATION of many data types. The SmartArt command, which is included on the Insert tab on the Ribbon, opens the Choose a SmartArt graphic dialog box in which you have to indicate what type of diagram you want to add. Diagrams have their own tab on the Options Ribbon with tools to edit them.

1. In a blank workbook, select cell **E5** as a destination for the graphics. Select the **Insert** tab on the **Ribbon** and click on the **Insert a SmartArt Graphic** tool in the **Illustrations** group.

2. All the types of diagrams that can be created in Excel are shown in the **Choose a SmartArt Graphic** dialog box. Click the **Cycle** option in the left pane.

3. From the layouts that correspond to this type of diagram, select the second one in the third line, **Radial Cycle**, and click **OK**.

4. The diagram is inserted in the sheet and the **Text** pane and the **SmartArt Tools** contextual tab open. Type **Neptune** in the first text box in the pane.

5. As you type, the text appears in the selected element of the diagram. Type **Proteus**, **Nereid**, **Larissa**, and **Galatea**, in the following text boxes.

In the preview section, you can see what the selected **SmartArt** graphic layout looks like and you also get a brief description of it.

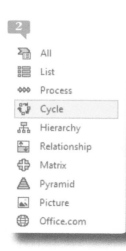

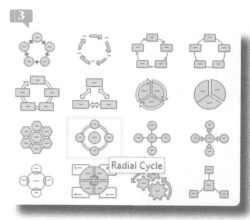

Excel offers a wide variety of types within each of the **SmartArt** diagram categories.

6. In order to add a shape to the diagram, click on the **Add Shape** tool in the **Create Graphic** group. 💬

7. A new element will appear in the diagram. Depending on the type of diagram, Excel allows you to add shapes behind, in front, over, or under the selected one. Type **Naiad** in the new shape. 💬

8. Save the workbook with the **Diagram** name in the **Documents** folder, on your computer.

9. Each element of the diagram (the shapes, the text, and the connecting lines) can be edited separately with its own editing tools, from the **Design** subtab. You will now change the diagram's colors. Click on the **Change Colors** button, in the **SmartArt Styles** group and select a multicolor combination. 💬

10. You will now apply a 3D style to the flowchart. Click on the **More** button from the **SmartArt Styles** gallery and select one in the **3-D** category. 💬

11. The commands of the **Format** subtab adapt to the element of the diagram that is selected. Select the subtab, click on the **Shape Fill** button in the **Shape Styles** group, and select one of the standard colors.

12. Pull down the **Shape Effects** menu, select the **Glow** option, and select one of its variations.

13. Remember that you can also edit the text contained in the elements of a diagram separately. Deselect it and save the changes.

055

IMPORTANT

You can fill each of the elements from your diagram with standard colors, pictures, gradient fills, or textures. Select the **No Fill** option to make them transparent.

The **Add Shape** button in the **Create Graphic** group adds new shapes to the diagram that correspond to the type of diagram that is being created.

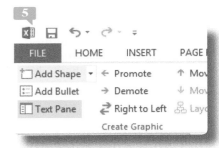

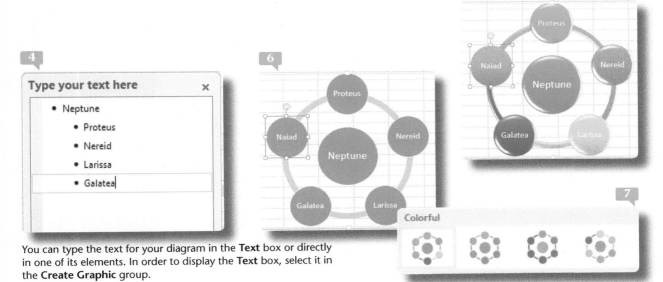

You can type the text for your diagram in the **Text** box or directly in one of its elements. In order to display the **Text** box, select it in the **Create Graphic** group.

Inserting headers and footers

IN THE TEXT GROUP ON THE INSERT TAB, you will find the Header & Footer tool. When you select it, the sheet displays the Page Layout view with the header selected and ready to be edited. Also, the Header & Footer tab, which allows you to edit the design of those elements, appears.

1. In this exercise, you will learn to add headers and footers to a spreadsheet. Select the **Insert** tab on the **Ribbon** and click on the **Header & Footer** tool in the **Text** group. 🔲¹

2. The view mode of the page changes automatically and the **Header & Footer Tools** contextual tab appears. The tools it offers allow you to select the field that you are going to include in the header or in the footer. Notice that the header is already displayed in editing mode. In order to see the built-in headers that are available in Excel, click on the **Header** button in the **Header & Footer** group. 🔲²

3. As you can see, you can show a lot of elements in the headers and the footers. Among them are the page number, the name

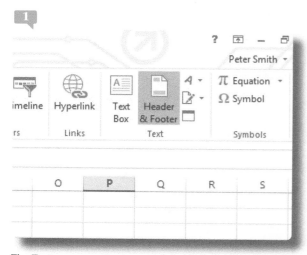

The **Text** group on the **Insert** tab holds the tools that allow you to automatically insert headers and footers in a spreadsheet.

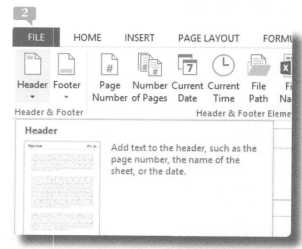

When you add a header or footer, the sheet is displayed in layout mode and a contextual tab appears with the editing tools for those elements.

056

and sheet of the workbook, its path, etc. Select the **Confidential; date; Page 1** option.

4. The headers and footers are texts and as such, can be edited with the usual program tools. Select an element of the header and select the **Design** subtab on the **Header & Footer Tools** tab.

5. Click on the **Go to Footer** tool in the **Navigation** group.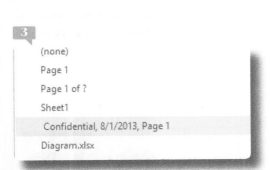

6. Click on the **Current Time** button in the **Header & Footer Elements** group.

7. Since the text box is now highlighted, you cannot see the current time, only the number for that element. In order to see the result, click on the box on the right of the footer.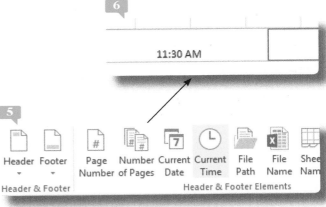

8. Creating headers and footers is not difficult at all. Click on a blank cell outside the header and footer editing mode.

9. In order to view the headers and footers, the program has to be in **Page Layout** view. Click on the first icon in the Workbook Views group on the **Status Bar** to select **Normal View**, and save the changes to finish the exercise.

When you insert a header or footer, the spreadsheet is displayed in **Layout View**. Use the icon on the **Status Bar** to go back to **Normal View**.

(none)
Page 1
Page 1 of ?
Sheet1
Confidential, 8/1/2013, Page 1
Diagram.xlsx

A large amount of preset headers and footers are available in Excel 2013. Select one of them from the **Header & Footer** group.

The buttons in the **Navigation** group allow you to quickly select the header or footer for a sheet.

You can insert elements such as the current date and time, etc., in the page header or footer.

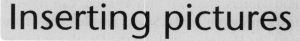

Inserting pictures

EXCEL ALLOWS YOU TO INSERT PICTURES in your spreadsheet. They can be clip art pictures found online or pictures that are stored on your computer.

1. Select a cell in a blank sheet, select the **Insert** tab, and click on the **Online Pictures** button in the **Illustrations** group. ▣

2. The **Insert Pictures** dialog box, which allows you to look for pictures online from different locations (the Office gallery, Bing, your Flickr account, or your SkyDrive space) opens. Click on the **Search** text box in the **Office.com Clip Art** option and type **home**.

3. Click on the **Search** icon to start the search. ▣

4. There are a lot of pictures displayed in the box. Hover over the results list with your mouse and place the cursor on one of them. Click on the magnifying glass icon that appears. ▣

5. The picture is shown in a bigger size, and you can see a summary of its properties. Click on the **Insert** button. ▣

6. The picture is inserted in the sheet and the **Picture Tools** contextual tab appears, with the necessary tools to modify its ap-

IMPORTANT

With the **Insert Pictures** dialog box, pictures from your Facebook account can be inserted directly into your worksheet.

Also insert from:

f

Use the **Online Pictures** button on the **Insert** tab to access the Insert Pictures box. Entering a keyword will make it easier to locate a specific type of picture.

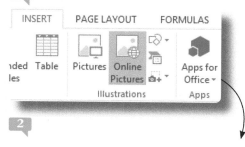

The **Office Clip Art** galleries include a large number of pictures organized by keywords.

pearance. You will practice with them in the next exercise. Select a blank cell, select the **Insert** tab and click on the **Pictures** button in the **Illustrations** group.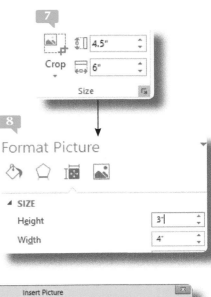

7. The **Insert Picture** window shows, by default, the contents of the **Pictures** folder. Locate the picture that you want to insert in your sheet (if you wish, you can use the **Sea.jpg** sample file that you will find in the download section on our website) and click the **Insert** button.

8. The picture is inserted in the sheet with its predetermined size. To size it, enter the new values directly in the **Shape Height** and **Shape Width** boxes in the **Size** group or by going to the **Format Picture** task pane. Click on the dialog box launcher in the **Size** group.

9. You will shrink the picture while locking the picture aspect ratio. Double-click in the **Height** text box in the **Size** section, insert **3** and press **Enter**.

10. You can use the **Format Picture** pane to edit more picture aspects (border, effects, fill, etc.). To finish this exercise, close this pane, deselect the picture, and save the file so that you can use it for the next exercise.

The picture contextual menu includes an option to access its Format task pane.

Editing pictures

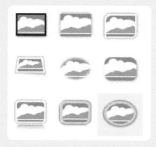

INCLUDING PICTURES ALLOWS you to enhance the design of spreadsheets and turns them into much more attractive, customized documents. There are many ways you can edit a picture, and you will learn about the most important ones in this exercise.

1. You will now edit the brightness, contrast, and sharpness of one of the pictures that you inserted in the previous exercise. Click on one of your pictures to select it and show the **Picture Tools** contextual tab.

2. Select the **Format** subtab and click on the **Corrections** command in the **Adjust** group. 🔲

3. Excel offers some preset brightness and contrast options with a live preview. Click once on the option you prefer from the drop-down menu.

4. With the **Color** button in the same **Tools** group you can color the picture and apply a grayscale or a sepia tone to it. Click that button and select the tone you prefer. 🔲²

You can use one of the options included in the **Corrections** command on the **Picture Tools** tab to change the picture's brightness, contrast, and sharpness.

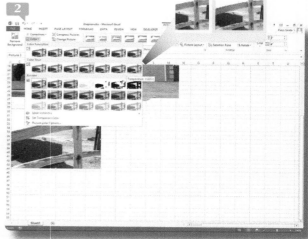

The **Recolor** command in the **Adjust** group unveils a drop-down menu that offers several color, tone, and saturation options.

058

5. You will now add a border to the picture. Click on the **Picture Border** command in the **Picture Styles** group, click on the **Weight** option, and select a **6 point** line. [3]

6. In order to change the border color, click on the **Picture Border** command again and select one of the colors from the **Standard color** palette.

7. You will now apply a soft edges effect to the picture that will clear the effect you had just added. Click on the **Picture Effects** command in the **Picture Styles** group. Click on the **Soft Edges** option and select one of the softest options so that you can notice the difference.

8. Select the **Remove Background** command in the **Adjust** group. [4]

9. The **Background Removal** tab gets automatically selected and part of the picture gets covered with a fuchsia layer. [5] This will be the part that will be removed. Select the **Mark Areas to Keep** command.

10. The cursor turns into a pencil with which you can select the areas of the picture you want to keep. Click on some of the dots on the fuchsia layer.

11. Notice how that increases the visible area of the picture. Click on the **Keep Changes** button and see the result. [6]

12. To finish the exercise, deselect the picture and save the changes you made to the sheet.

The **Remove Background** command triggers the **Background Removal** tab whose tools allow you to clear parts of the picture while keeping only the ones you want.

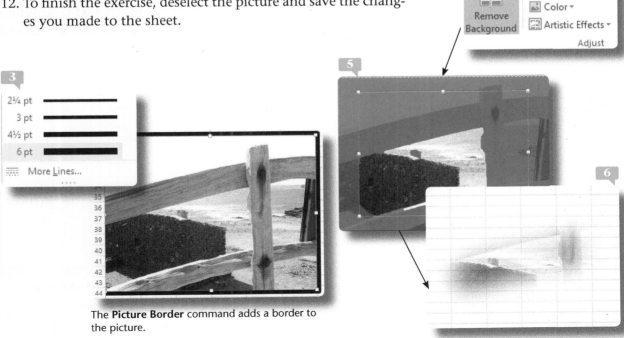

The **Picture Border** command adds a border to the picture.

Inserting WordArt

IMPORTANT

In order to remove the WordArt design from a text, use the **Clear WordArt** option that you will find in the Designs gallery.

THE WORDART FUNCTION IS AVAILABLE IN MOST of the applications that are a part of the Office suite. It is both a text and a design function. The WordArt gallery contains a large variety of shapes and styles that can be inserted into sheets and then edited later on.

1. You will find the tools you need to insert WordArt text on the **Insert** tab, on the **Ribbon,** and you will find the ones that allow you to edit this item on the **Format** subtab of the **Drawing** tools contextual tab. Select an empty cell in your sheet, select the **Insert** tab, and click on the **Insert WordArt** button in the **Text** group. 🗨1

2. Select the last one in the third row from the **WordArt Styles** gallery that pops up. 🗨2

3. The **Your text here** sample message appears in the center of the sheet, formatted in the WordArt style you chose. Type your text, for example **Menorca**, in the assigned location, and double-click on it to select it. 🗨3

4. Place the cursor on one of the edges of the text box. When the shape of the cursor changes to four arrows, click and hold

The **Insert WordArt** command can be found in the **Text** group on the **Insert** tab. When you click on it, you will see a drop-down menu containing a styles gallery, and you can choose the style you prefer.

When you select The **WordArt style**, a sample text appears, and you have to replace it with your own text.

059

down the mouse and drag the text to the desired location. After that, you can release the mouse button.

5. The **Drawing Tools** group allows you to modify the fill color and the text outline, and to apply special effects to it; these actions can also be carried out from the **Format Shape** pane. Click on the **WordArt Styles** group dialog box launcher and select the first section in this box, **Text Fill & Outline**.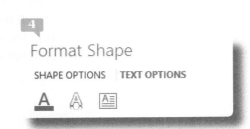

6. Pull down the **Text Fill** section, select the **Gradient fill** option, and pull down the list of preset gradients.

7. Select one of the samples and check the result.

8. You will now apply a reflection effect to the text. Click on the **Text Effects** command, which looks like an A with a glow effect, click on the **Reflection** option, and select one of the preset reflection variations.

9. You will now select another one of the available **WordArt** styles. Click on the **More** button in the **WordArt Styles** gallery and select one of them.

10. You can create spectacular, eye-catching text with very little effort thanks to the **WordArt** tool. Deselect the text and save the changes to finish the exercise.

You can change a WordArt style for another one at any time by going to the **WordArt gallery** or by editing the different elements of the text to your liking.

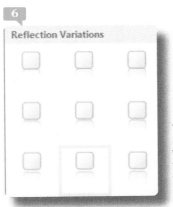

You can apply effects such as shadows, reflections, glows, bevels, etc., to a **WordArt** text just as if it were a picture. You can find all those effects in the **Text Effects** command in the **WordArt Styles** group.

Creating and editing links

A LINK IS A REFERENCE TO ANOTHER WORKBOOK, another cell, or another program. The main advantage of links is that they are updated. A linked object is an object created in a file, called a source file, which is then inserted into a destination file while a connection remains between the two of them.

1. In this exercise, you will use two different books: **Points3.xlsx** and **Autofilter.xlsx**. Make sure that both files are open. If they are not, open them from the **File** tab.

2. You will now link a cell on one sheet to another cell in the same workbook. Select cell **B2** from the **Points3** workbook and click on the **Copy** command in the **Clipboard** group on the **Home** tab. 💬

3. Create a fourth sheet in the workbook and select cell **B1**.

4. Go to the paste options. Pull down the **Paste** menu and select the **Paste Link** option from the Paste drop-down menu, which is the second icon in the **Other Paste Options** section. 💬

5. Look at the **Formula Bar**. 💬 The name of the sheet and the source cell that you just linked the selected cell to appear on it. In order to link cells from different sheets of the same workbook, you have to specify the formula's variables and refer to

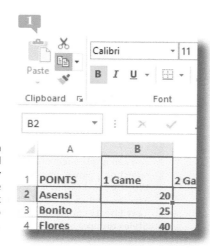

Select a cell with contents and use the **Copy** command or the **Ctrl+C** shortcut keys to copy it to the clipboard.

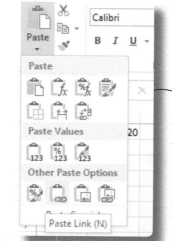

=Sheet1!$B$2

When you paste the contents of a copied cell to use them as a link, the **Formula Bar** shows a reference to that source cell.

060

the cell that is on the other sheet with the following syntax: **nameofthesheet!cellreference.** You are now going to make sure you have really linked the sheets. Select **Sheet1** by clicking on its label.

6. You will now change the value of the source cell to see if the linked cell updates its contents. Double-click on cell **B2**, type **35**, and press **Enter.**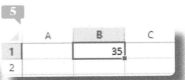

7. Select **Sheet4** again and look at the linked cell.

8. Its contents are the same as those of the source cell. You will now link a cell from this workbook with one from another workbook. Click on the **View** tab, click the **Switch Windows** button, and select the **AutoFilter** workbook by clicking on its name.

9. Click on cell **B2** and use the **Ctrl + C** shortcut to copy it.

10. You will now go back to the **Points3** workbook. Pull down the **Switch Windows** menu again and select this workbook.

11. Paste the contents you copied to use them as a link. In order to do that, go to the **Home** tab, pull down the **Paste** menu, and select the **Paste Link** option.

12. Now look at the **Formula Bar.** You may want to check that both cells are linked by going back to the other workbook and editing the source cell. Press the **Escape** key to empty the **Clipboard** and save the changes.

	A	B	C
1	POINTS	1 Game	2 Game	3 Ga
2	Asensi	35	15
3	Bonito	25	25
4	Flores	40	30
5	Álvarez	10	25
6	Vera	60	10
7	Nerín	30	25
8	Balaguer	25	45
9	Pérez	25	55
10	Smith	30	25

	A	B	C
1		35	
2			

After linking two cells from different sheets, edit the contents of the source cell and make sure that the contents of the destination cell get updated.

Use the **Switch Windows** command on the **View** tab to switch from one workbook to another when several are open.

=[Autofilter.xlsx]Sheet1!$B$2

Look at the formula that appears on the **Formula Bar** when you link cells from different workbooks.

133

Creating and selecting hyperlinks

HYPERLINKS, WHICH ARE OFTEN USED on websites, have been transferred to modern office computing applications such as the ones included in Microsoft Office. A hyperlink is a link that directly connects with another point of the same workbook or with another file. This file can be created by another application; thus, when clicking on this type of hyperlink, the file will automatically open along with the application that manages it.

1. Begin by creating a hyperlink in a cell that will be linked to another cell in this same sheet. Select the **C3** cell on Sheet1 of the **Points3** workbook, select the **Insert** tab and click on the **Hyperlink** button. 🔲

2. This opens the **Insert Hyperlink** dialog box that displays, by default, the contents of the **My Documents** folder. This folder belongs to the existing file or web page category, as you can see in the **Link to** section. However, in this case, try to create a link between two cells in the same sheet. Click on the **Place in This Document** category. 🔲

3. The cells in the workbook are now displayed and you can select any of them and define the reference for the cell with which you wish to link it. By default, Excel offers the A1

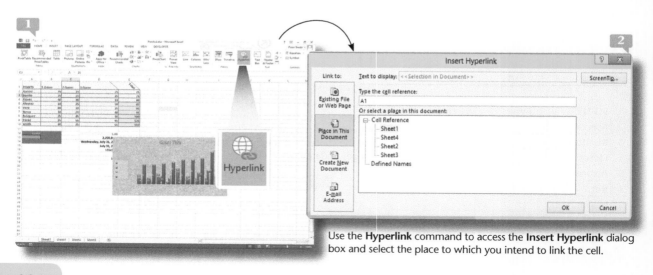

Use the **Hyperlink** command to access the **Insert Hyperlink** dialog box and select the place to which you intend to link the cell.

061

cell in Sheet1. Type the name of a cell in the **Type the cell reference** field and, after selecting another sheet other than the currently active one, 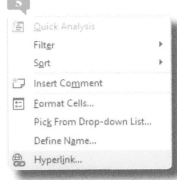 click on the **OK** button.

4. The contents of the selected cell appear underlined and in blue. This is a characteristic of hyperlinks and it helps you identify them. Excel provides information on created hyperlinks and their destination through pop-up tabs that appear when floating the cursor over the hyperlinks. Try it and then click on the cell to go to the destination cell.

5. You will now create another type of hyperlink, one that links to data in a different workbook other than the one that contains the link. Right-click on the **D7** cell and select the **Hyperlink** option in the pop-up menu.

6. Back in the **Insert Hyperlink** dialog box, click on the **Existing File or Web Page** category, locate and select the **Autofilter** file, and click on the **OK** button.

7. In order to check if it works, click on the blue hyperlink to open the book to which it is associated.

The book to which you have linked the cell opens. Remember that you can also add hyperlinks to documents created with other applications.

IMPORTANT

When creating a hyperlink, the link is displayed in blue to help you find it. Once you have clicked on it, the hyperlink becomes purple when the default Windows 8 settings are active.

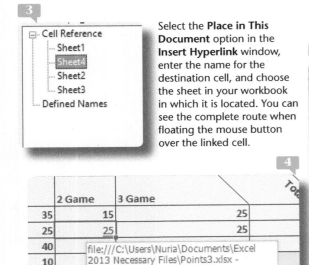

Select the **Place in This Document** option in the **Insert Hyperlink** window, enter the name for the destination cell, and choose the sheet in your workbook in which it is located. You can see the complete route when floating the mouse button over the linked cell.

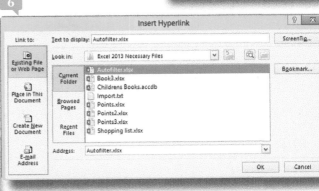

You can create hyperlinks to point to the same document, to other documents created with Excel, or other programs or e-mail addresses.

Inserting linked objects

OBJECTS ARE FILES SUCH AS TEXT, audio or picture files, etc. Inserting a linked object means that it will be automatically modified in the destination file whenever it is changed in its original location.

1. In this exercise you will insert a linked object in a spreadsheet. You'll work with a text document, called **The Odyssey.docx**, which you can download from our website. Once you have the file saved on your computer, click on an empty cell in the **Autofilter** workbook, enable the **Insert** tab, and click on the **Object** command, in the **Text** tool group.

2. The **Object** dialog box shows two tabs. The **Create New** tab displays a series of file types for the user to choose. Once you have selected any of these options, Excel will open the appropriate application to create the selected file type from scratch. In this case, link to an existing file. Click on the **Create from File** tab.

3. Look for the file that will be linked. To do so, click on the **Browse** button.

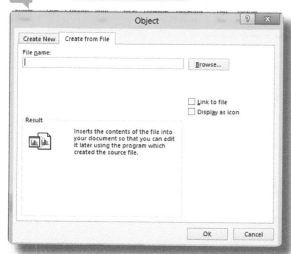

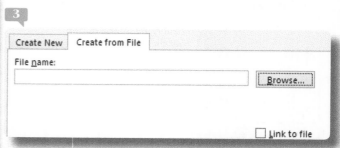

Open the **Object** dialog box using the button with the same name in the **Text** tool group, in the **Insert** tab. Then go to the **Create from File** tab in this window and use the **Browse** button to locate the file to be inserted.

4. Excel opens the **Browse** window, displaying the contents of the **Documents** folder. Locate and select the **The Odyssey.docx** file and click on the **Insert** button.

5. Back in the **Object** dialog box, in the space reserved for the file name, you can see the location of the selected document. Check to see if the object is linked to the original file. To do so, check the verification box in the **Link to file** option.

6. The **Display as icon** option inserts the object as an icon. Keep this option disabled and click on the **OK** button.

7. The linked file has been inserted in the selected cell of the open workbook. Notice that the **Drawing Tools** contextual tab has been enabled, which indicates that the object was inserted as a drawing. Save your changes by clicking on the **Save** icon in the **Quick Access Toolbar**.

You can complete the exercise by opening the document you inserted as an object in your spreadsheet and making some changes to it to see that the changes are applied automatically.

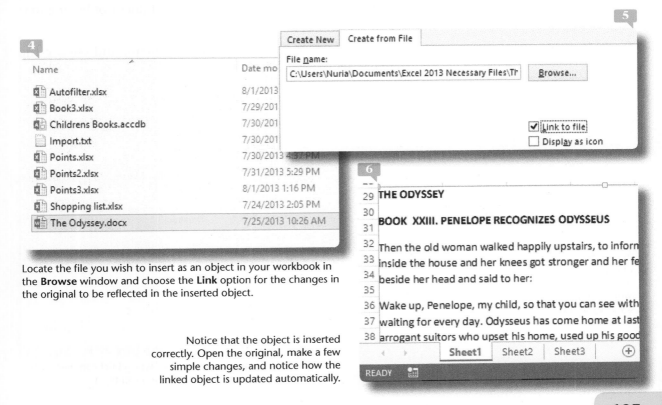

Locate the file you wish to insert as an object in your workbook in the **Browse** window and choose the **Link** option for the changes in the original to be reflected in the inserted object.

Notice that the object is inserted correctly. Open the original, make a few simple changes, and notice how the linked object is updated automatically.

Creating and using ranges

RANGES ARE GROUPS OF CONSECUTIVE or separate cells in a spreadsheet. Creating and naming ranges is very useful in creating formulas. The range name becomes one more operand that includes the contents of all its cells.

1. Click on the **A1** cell in **Sheet1** of the **Points3** workbook, press the **Shift** key and, holding it down, select the **D6** cell. 🔲

2. To name a range you can use the **Define name** option in its pop-up menu or the tool with the same name in the **Formulas** tab. Enable it and click on the **Define Name** button in the **Defined Names** group. 🔲

3. Specify the range, the field to which it belongs, and the cells it refers to in the **New Name** field. 🔲 Type **eliminated** in the **Name** field and click on the **OK** button.

4. The **eliminated** name appears in the **Name Box**, 🔲 as that range is still selected. Click on a cell that does not belong to it to unselect it.

5. Select the **A25** cell, open its pop-up menu, and choose the **Define Name** option. 🔲

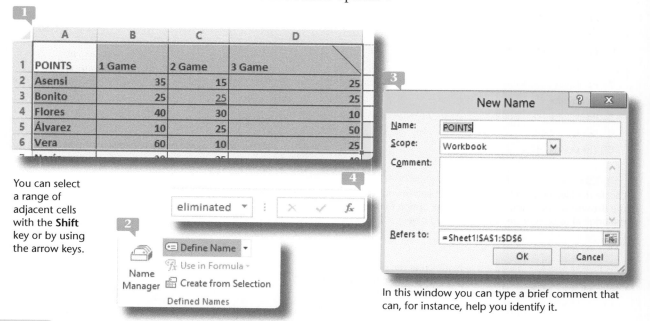

You can select a range of adjacent cells with the **Shift** key or by using the arrow keys.

	A	B	C	D
1	POINTS	1 Game	2 Game	3 Game
2	Asensi	35	15	25
3	Bonito	25	25	25
4	Flores	40	30	10
5	Álvarez	10	25	50
6	Vera	60	10	25

eliminated

Define Name
Use in Formula
Name Manager   Create from Selection
Defined Names

New Name

Name: POINTS
Scope: Workbook
Comment:

Refers to: =Sheet1!$A$1:$D$6

OK   Cancel

In this window you can type a brief comment that can, for instance, help you identify it.

6. Back in the **New Name** window, define the cells the range will refer to. Click on the icon to the right of the **Refers to** field.

7. The dialog box is reduced so you can directly select the appropriate cells from the sheet. Press the **Shift** key and, without releasing it, click on the **B26** cell.

8. In order to maximize the dialog box, click on the icon to the right of the cell combination again.

9. Click on the **Name** field, type **winners**, and click **OK** to apply the name to the range.

10. In order to check if the name has been applied correctly, press the **Shift** key and, without releasing it, click on the **B26** cell.

11. Click on the arrow next to the name window to open the list of ranges and select the one called **eliminated**.

12. Create a formula by using ranges. Select an empty cell, type in the formula =**E5+E6+E7+F5+F6+F7** and press **Enter**.

13. Create a range that includes the cells that belong to this formula. Click on the **Define Name** tool and, in the **Name** field, type **one**.

14. Click on the icon that appears next to the **Refers to** field to minimize the dialog box, select the **E5** cell, press the **Shift** key and, without releasing it, click on the **F7** cell.

15. Maximize the **New Name** window and click on the **OK** button.

16. Select another cell, enter the same formula as the previous one by typing =**SUM(one)** and press **Enter**.

17. The result is the same. Creating cell ranges helps you enter complex formulas that require several cells, either contiguous or separate. Click on the **Save** icon on the **Quick Access Toolbar**.

IMPORTANT

Excel assigns, by default, the contents of the first cell, if it is text, as the name for a cell range.

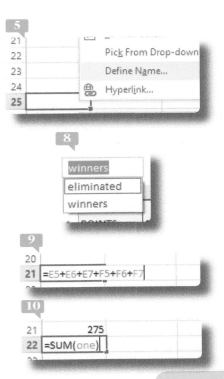

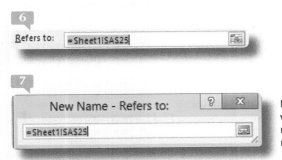

Minimize the **New Name** window to directly select the range of cells you are going to name directly from the sheet.

Calculating with functions

IMPORTANT

Excel 2013 includes a large amount of new functions, most of which belong to the trigonometry, mathematic, engineering, and web categories. Experiment using these new functions by using the help menu.

FUNCTIONS ARE DEFAULT FORMULAS that execute complex operations with an established syntax. Excel has a large amount of automatic functions divided into categories, such as mathematical, logical, text, or date and time functions. All functions have a name such as SUM, and some elements between brackets and separated by a semicolon. These brackets are essential even in those functions that do not require arguments.

1. Apply the **SUM** function to the **Points3** file using the Formula window. Select an empty cell and click on the **Insert Function** tool, in the **Function Library** tools group in the **Formulas** tab.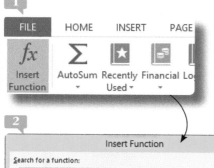

2. This opens the **Insert Function** dialog box in which you can select the appropriate function for each case. In this case, choose the **SUM** function and click on the **OK** button.

3. Excel proposes the cells to be added in the **Function Arguments** window. Move the cursor to the **Number1** argument box and, if necessary, minimize the box by clicking on the red arrow icon to the right of this field.

4. Select a cell with contents in your sheet, for instance, the **E4** cell, and maximize the **Function Arguments** window.

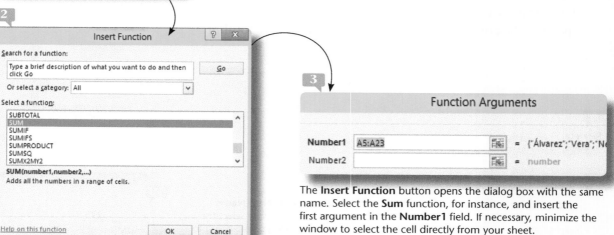

The **Insert Function** button opens the dialog box with the same name. Select the **Sum** function, for instance, and insert the first argument in the **Number1** field. If necessary, minimize the window to select the cell directly from your sheet.

5. The reference of this cell has been entered in the first argument box. Enter a range in the second argument field. Click on this field and type one, which is the range name you created in the previous exercise.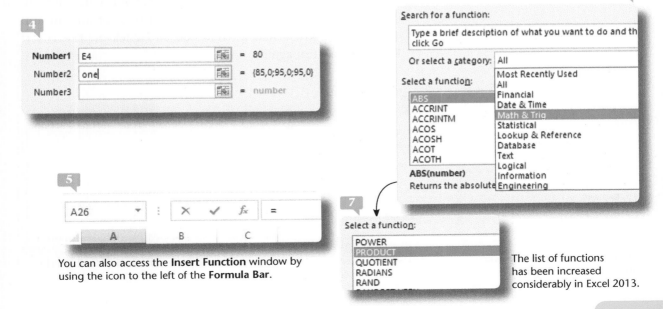

6. When inserting the second number, the values that make up the range are displayed next to its name. Click on the **OK** button.

7. Following the same procedure, create a formula that multiplies the contents of two cells. Select an empty cell and open the **Insert Function** window by clicking on the **Insert Function** button, to the left of the **Formula Bar**.

8. Click on the arrow to the right of the **Or select a category** field in the **Insert Function** dialog box and choose the **Math & Trig** option.

9. Choose **PRODUCT** in the **Select a function** field and click on the **OK** button.

10. As with the **SUM** function, choose a cell for the **Number1** field and another for the **Number2** field.

11. Click on the **OK** button and notice that the cell contains the result of the multiplication of those two cells.

You can also insert functions using the ones grouped by categories in the **Function** library.

064

IMPORTANT

In the **Financial** category you can find functions related to payments, prices, benefits, income, etc., and in the **Logical** category you can find true or false, yes or no, or error functions.

AND
FALSE
IF
IFERROR
IFNA
NOT
OR

It's possible to include one function as an argument for another. In this case, they are called **nested functions**.

Number1   E4   = 80
Number2   one   = {85,0;95,0;95,0}
Number3   = number

Search for a function:

Type a brief description of what you want to do and then click Go

Or select a category: All

Select a function:

ABS
ACCRINT
ACCRINTM
ACOS
ACOSH
ACOT
ACOTH

ABS(number)
Returns the absolute

Most Recently Used
All
Financial
Date & Time
Math & Trig
Statistical
Lookup & Reference
Database
Text
Logical
Information
Engineering

A26   :   ×   ✓   *fx*   =

A   B   C

You can also access the **Insert Function** window by using the icon to the left of the **Formula Bar**.

Select a function:

POWER
PRODUCT
QUOTIENT
RADIANS
RAND

The list of functions has been increased considerably in Excel 2013.

Calculating with mathematical functions

MATHEMATICAL FUNCTIONS ARE the most widely used for constructing formulas. Most tables that people create are basically built by using the sum and product functions. The Help window gives an explanation of each function and what variables are needed.

1. In this exercise you will learn how to use mathematical functions. Select a free cell and click on the **Insert Function** button in the **Formulas** tab.

2. Click on the arrow button in the **Or select a category** field and choose the **Math&Trig** option.

3. Locate and select the **POWER** function 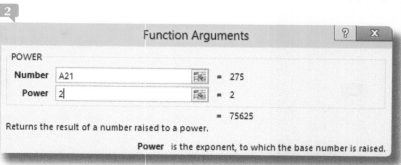 and click **OK**.

4. This opens the Help window that will assist you when entering functions. Enter the number you wish to square. Minimize the Function Arguments box by clicking on the button located to the right of the **Number** field, select a cell and maximize the box.

5. See the results of squaring a number. Enter the number **2** in the **Power** field and click **OK**.

6. The process is done and the formula is set. For the next formula, find a function that rounds a number to a certain amount of decimal points. Select a free cell and click on the **Insert Function** button again.

1

```
Select a function:
PI
POWER
PRODUCT
QUOTIENT
RADIANS
RAND
RANDBETWEEN

POWER(number,power)
```

Open the **Insert Formula** window and select **Math&Trig** in the categories list.

2

Function Arguments		?	X

POWER

Number	A21	= 275
Power	2	= 2

= 75625

Returns the result of a number raised to a power.

Power is the exponent, to which the base number is raised.

You will see the contents of the cell whose name you entered in the **Number** field. Below, you will see the results of the operation.

7. Use the vertical scroll bar to locate the **Round** function, select it, and click on the **OK** button.

8. Select a free cell in your sheet, for instance, **B12**, to enter it as the first argument in the function, click on the second argument box, **Num_digits**, type **2**, and click on the **OK** button.

9. You will now see how the formula works. Select the cell you have set as the first argument (**B12**), enter a number with three decimal points, and press the **Enter** key.

10. You will now calculate the surface of a circle. The formula to do so is **a=π.r²** (pi times radius squared). Therefore, you will use two nested functions. Select a free cell, click on the **Insert Function** button in the **Formula Bar**, locate and select the **Product** function, and click on the **OK** button.

11. For this exercise, you will calculate the surface of a circle whose radius is 60. Delete the contents of the **Number1** field by pressing the **Delete** key and enter the **B6** cell number, which contains the value **60**.

12. Type a circumflex accent followed by 2, click on the argument **Number2**, type **PI** followed by two parentheses, one opened and one closed, and click OK.

13. When working on your own, and depending on the type of calculations you want to use, Excel 2013 guides you in creating the formulas through the Help window and dialog boxes. Click on the **Save** button in the **Quick Access Toolbar**.

IMPORTANT

Some of the new mathematical and trigonometric functions in Excel 2013 are the following: **ACOT**, to return the co-tangent arc to a number; **ARABIC**, to convert a Roman numeral to an Arabic numeral; **BITAND**, to obtain a "bitwise and" of two numbers; and **CEILING.MATH**, to round a number up to the nearest integer or multiple of significance.

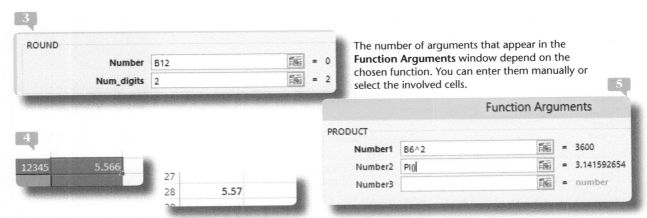

The number of arguments that appear in the **Function Arguments** window depend on the chosen function. You can enter them manually or select the involved cells.

The **Round** function has rounded a number with three decimal points to only two.

Using text functions

IMPORTANT

The **VALUE** functions are a new feature in Excel 2013: **NUMBER** converts text to numbers independently from regional settings, **UNICODE** returns the number that corresponds to the first character in the text, and **UNICHAR**, with which you practiced in this exercise.

SOME TEXT FUNCTIONS ONLY return referenced figures such as the code for a character (code), or the other way around (character), which yields the character that corresponds to a number or code between 1 and 255. Some others are very useful to carry out searches or to count characters (find, search, and replace). Finally, you can access functions that manipulate text, such as concatenate (joins two chains of text), upper, lower and spaces.

1. All computer programs work with a map of 255 characters, each of which corresponds to a number. Excel text functions allow you to discover which number corresponds to every character and vice versa. Select an empty cell, click on the **Insert function** icon in the **Formula Bar**, enable the **Text** category, select the **Code** function, and click **OK**. 🔲

2. Select a cell with text in it in the **Function Arguments** window, which you can minimize by clicking on the contract icon, and click **OK**. 🔲

3. The function returns the code that corresponds to the first letter of the text, in this case 83. You will now practice using the **Upper** function. Select an empty cell and click on the **Insert function** icon in the **Formula Bar**.

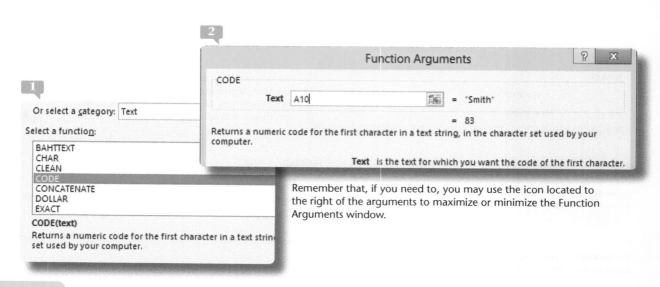

Remember that, if you need to, you may use the icon located to the right of the arguments to maximize or minimize the Function Arguments window.

4. Select the **UPPER** text function and click on the **OK** button.

5. Select another cell with text content in the **Text** field and click **OK**.

6. The cell that includes the function presents the same characters as the selected one but in uppercase letters. You will now work with a new text function in Excel 2013, the **UNICHAR** function, which returns a specified numeric value to a specific unicode character. Select an empty cell, open the **Insert Function** window, and locate and select **UNICHAR**.

7. Click on the **OK** button.

8. This function only has one compulsory argument, the one you wish to convert to a unicode character. Enter the value **(0)** in the **Number** field and click on the **OK** button.

9. Notice the value returned by the cell in which you have inserted the function. In this case, the value **(0)** corresponds to the error value **#VALUE!** Delete the contents of this cell and finish the exercise by clicking on the **Save** icon in the **Quick Access Toolbar** to save your changes.

Keep in mind that the results of the formulas and some of the functions in Excel may vary between x86 and x86-64 bit computers and Windows RT computers with ARM architecture.

066

Select a function:

T
TEXT
TRIM
UNICHAR
UNICODE
UPPER
VALUE

The **UPPER** function converts a text chain into capital letters.

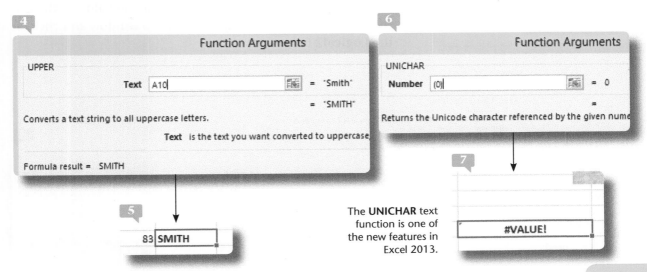

Function Arguments

UPPER

Text A10 = "Smith"

= "SMITH"

Converts a text string to all uppercase letters.

Text is the text you want converted to uppercase.

Formula result = SMITH

83 SMITH

Function Arguments

UNICHAR

Number (0) = 0

=

Returns the Unicode character referenced by the given nume

#VALUE!

The **UNICHAR** text function is one of the new features in Excel 2013.

Using logical functions

THERE ARE NINE LOGICAL FUNCTIONS. FALSE returns the logical false value, and TRUE returns the logical true value. The function is executed if an action fulfills a condition; the IFERROR function returns a value if the expression is an error and the value of the expression is not. The function NOT invert the logic of an argument, the function OR returns true if an argument is, and the AND function returns true if all arguments are. The new IFNO function returns the specified value if the expression becomes a #N/A and it does not return the result of the expression, and the new XOR function returns an logical exclusive OR for all arguments.

1. Create a formula that returns the true or false value for an assertion. Type **3** and **4**, respectively, 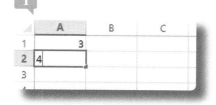 in the **A1** and **A2** cells of a blank sheet. Select the **B7** cell and open the **Insert Function** window.

2. Since you want both arguments of the assertion to be fulfilled simultaneously, use the **AND** function. Select the **Logical** category in the **Or select a category** window, select **AND**, and click **OK**. 🄳

3. If you need to, minimize the Help window by clicking on the button to the right of the **Logical1** field, select the **A1** cell, and type **<5**.

4. The first condition to be fulfilled is that the value of the cell should be less than 5. Maximize the Help window and click on the **Logical2** field.

	A	B	C
1	3		
2	4		
3			

Search for a function:

Type a brief description of what you want to do and then click Go

Or select a category: Logical

Select a function:

AND
FALSE
IF
IFERROR
IFNA
NOT
OR

AND

Logical1	A1<5		= TRUE
Logical2	A2>2		= TRUE
Logical3			= logical

After selecting an empty cell, open the **Insert Function** window and select the category and the function you need.

146

067

5. Minimize the dialog box, select the **A2** cell, type **>2**, maximize the window, and click on the **OK** button.

6. The cell in which you entered the function presents the value **TRUE**. See what happens if one of the logical values established in the function is not fulfilled. Select the **A1** cell, type **6**, and press **Enter**.

7. The contents of the **B7** cell now present the value **FALSE**. You will now use the **IF** function. Select the **B8** cell and click on the **Insert Function** button in the **Formula Bar**.

8. Select the **IF** logical function and click **OK**.

9. Once again, the referenced cells will be **A1** and **A2**. What you want to find out is if the contents of the first cell are greater than those of the second. Type **A1>A2** in the **Logical_test** field.

10. Enter the value that the function must return in the event that the condition is fulfilled. Click on the **Value_if_true** field and type **correct**.

11. Define the value the function must return if the condition is not fulfilled. Locate the cursor in the **value_if_false** field, type **incorrect**, and click **OK**.

12. The condition is true because the value expressed in cell **B8** is correct. Try it. Select the **A1** cell, type **2**, and press **Enter**.

13. See how the value **incorrect** appears in cell **B8**. Finish the exercise by saving your changes.

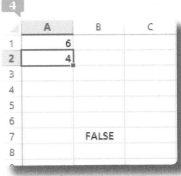

If the two conditions established in the **AND** function are not fulfilled, Excel returns the word **FALSE**.

In this example, if the condition established in the logical test field is fulfilled, that is, if the value of cell A1 is greater than the value of cell A2, Excel will give you the message **correct**, whereas, if it isn't, it will give you the message **incorrect**.

Function Arguments

IF

Logical_test   A1>A2   = TRUE

Value_if_true   "correct"   = "correct"

Value_if_false incorrect   =

                                     = "correct"

Checks whether a condition is met, and returns one value if TRUE, and another value if

Value_if_false is the value that is returned if Logical_test is F is returned.

Using references

IN ORDER TO CREATE TRULY USEFUL TABLES that carry out calculations on their own, the tables must include formulas that link cells to each other. References can be relative (A1), absolute ($A$1), or mixed ($A1 or $1).

1. In the **Points3** data table, insert a column after the E column with the same format; then select the **F1** cell, type **1st Part**, and press **Enter**.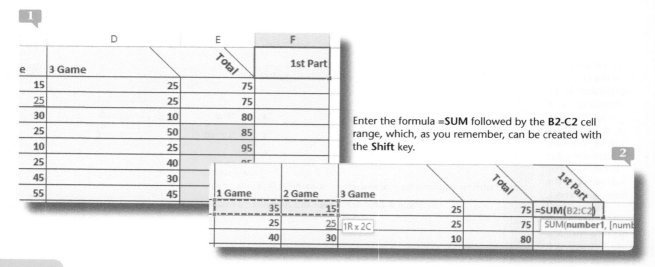

2. The data in this new column will be the result of adding the two first parts. Thus, in the case of the first player, the formula will add the values of the **B2-C2** range. Click on the **AutoSum** tool, in the **Function Library** group, select the cell **B2**, press the **Shift** key and, holding it down, click on the **C2** cell to create the range. Click on the **Enter** button in the **Formula Bar**.

3. You are now in the **F2** cell and you can see the formula assigned to it. The remaining cells in the **1st Part** column will need to be filled in with formulas that are identical to this one but with the row numbers corresponding to each one. Press the **Ctrl + C** shortcut to copy the contents of this cell to the clipboard, select the cell immediately below this one and press the **Ctrl + V** shortcut.

Enter the formula =SUM followed by the **B2-C2** cell range, which, as you remember, can be created with the **Shift** key.

148

4. Excel understands that, being a relative reference copied to a lower row, all references to rows must increase by one. Select the **F4** cell and press **Ctrl + V** again. 3️⃣

5. Make each player's score a percentage of the total points of all players. To do so, you must calculate that value and create a new column in which these percentages will be calculated. Select the **G1** cell, type **% Total**, and press **Enter**.

6. Select the **E11** cell, type **Grand total**, and press the right arrow key.

7. Enter the required function to obtain the total score of all players. Enter the function **=SUM(E2:E10)** 4️⃣ in the active cell and press the **Enter** key.

8. Begin by entering the multiplication of the total amount of points of the first player (**E2** cell) by **100**. Click on the **G2** cell and type **=E2*100**.

9. Divide the total of this operation by the contents of the **F11** cell, which contains the total of all players. Type **/$F$11** (the dollar sign indicates that it is an absolute reference) 5️⃣ and press **Enter**.

10. Since the first reference is relative and the second one is absolute, if you copy this formula and paste the first reference in another cell it will adapt to its new location, whereas the second will remain static. Press the **Ctrl + C** shortcut to copy the contents of this cell, select the **G3** cell, press the **Ctrl + V** shortcut and see the formula that appears in the **Formula Bar**. 6️⃣

068

IMPORTANT

References to cells in other workbooks are called **external links** or **references**.

4️⃣

25	75	50
10	80	70
50	85	
25	95	
40	95	
30	100	
45	125	
55	110	
Grand total	=SUM(E2:E10	

This function will add the contents of the cells from E2 to E10.

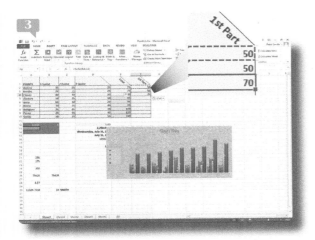

3️⃣

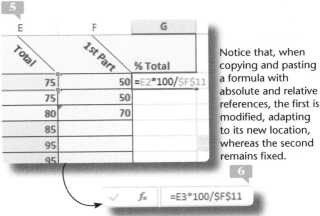

5️⃣

E	F	G
Total	1st Part	% Total
75	50	=E2*100/$F$11
75	50	
80	70	
85		
95		
95		

Notice that, when copying and pasting a formula with absolute and relative references, the first is modified, adapting to its new location, whereas the second remains fixed.

6️⃣

fx =E3*100/$F$11

149

Working with precedence

IMPORTANT

In **Excel Help** you will find a list of all operators, which includes a description and examples for each one. You can also find a table of **operator priorities** in the **General information** on **Formulas** section.

THE TERM PRECEDENCE INDICATES the order in which calculations in a formula are carried out if the formula has several operators. Excel will first calculate the operations between brackets, and the remaining operations will be carried out in order according to the list of operator priorities. If a formula contains operators with the same order of precedence, they will be calculated from left to right. Remember: you need to keep in mind the order in which you place operators and operands. If you are unsure about the order, you can use brackets even if they are not necessary.

1. Continue working on the **Points3** workbook. Select an empty cell, type **=5*4+6**, and press the **Enter** key.

2. In another free cell, type **=5*(4+6)** and press the **Enter** key again.

3. The first formula has multiplied **5 by 4** and has added **6** to the result. The second formula, on the other hand, first carried out the operation between brackets and then multiplied the result by 5. Thus, including brackets in the second formula has proved decisive. Enter a formula that refers to cells with contents. Type **=B2/C3^2** in an empty cell and press **Enter**.

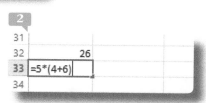

30	11309.7336		83	**SMITH**
31				
32	=5*4+6			

The results of these two operations will be different due to the fact that, as it establishes precedence, Excel carries out the operations between brackets first.

31		
32	26	
33	=5*(4+6)	
34		

30	11309.7336		83	**SMITH**
31				
32	26			
33	50			
34	=B2/C3^2			
35				

Precedence also affects references to cells. In this case, according to Excel's criteria of precedence, the exponent will be calculated first, and then divided by the contents of the first operator.

4. The formula you entered divides the contents in a cell by the contents in another squared. Following the strict hierarchical order of the operators, the exponential has been calculated before the division. If you want the exponential of the result of the division, you must use brackets. Select the last modified cell and, in the **Formula Bar**, change the formula to =(B2/C3)^2 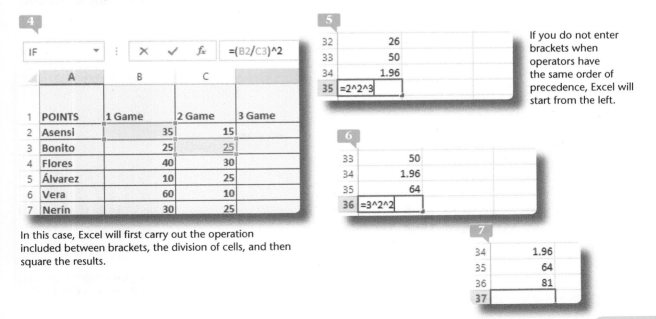 and press **Enter**.

5. The result is different. See what happens when the operators have the same rank of precedence. Type =2^2^3 in another empty cell and press the **Enter** key.

6. The operation to the left is carried out first, as 2 squared is 4 which, cubed, yields 64. To check the calculation process of the operation, enter the same formula with the order altered. Type =3^2^2 in another cell and press the **Enter** key.

7. The result is **81**, as 3 squared is 9, which, squared, is 81. Finish the exercise by clicking on the **Save** icon in the **Quick Access Toolbar**.

069

4

IF	fx	=(B2/C3)^2

	A	B	C	
1	POINTS	1 Game	2 Game	3 Game
2	Asensi	35	15	
3	Bonito	25	25	
4	Flores	40	30	
5	Álvarez	10	25	
6	Vera	60	10	
7	Nerín	30	25	

In this case, Excel will first carry out the operation included between brackets, the division of cells, and then square the results.

5

32	26	
33	50	
34	1.96	
35	=2^2^3	

If you do not enter brackets when operators have the same order of precedence, Excel will start from the left.

6

33	50	
34	1.96	
35	64	
36	=3^2^2	

7

34	1.96	
35	64	
36	81	
37		

Precedent and dependent cells

PRECEDENT CELLS ARE CELLS THAT REFER to the formulas in other cells. Dependent cells are those that contain formulas that refer to other cells. Assume the A1 cell contains the formula =C8; in that case, cell C8 would be the precedent cell, whereas cell A1 would be the dependent cell.

1. In this exercise you will learn about the usefulness of some of the commands included in the **Formula Auditing** group, in the **Formulas** tab on the **Ribbon**. The commands in this group allow you to display the link between cells with formulas on the sheet. Select a cell on your sheet that contains a formula that refers to other cells.

2. Click on the **Trace Precedents** command in the **Formula Auditing** group. **1**

3. Excel automatically draws blue arrows stemming from the selected cell that go to the cells on which it depends. **2** In the **Formula Bar**, check to see which cells they are. You can also carry out the reverse operation, that is, to graphically show the formulas that provide a cell with data, that is, dependent cells. Click on one of the cells to which a formula in another cell refers to.

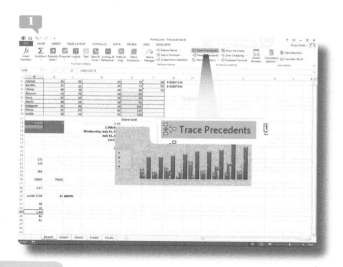

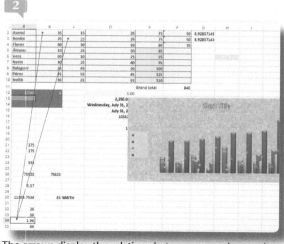

The arrows display the relations between precedent and dependent cells.

070

4. Click on the **Trace Dependents** command in the **Formula Auditing** group. 3

5. In this case, the blue arrows indicate cells in which the selected cell participates. You can check directly by clicking on each one of these cells and reading the formula in the **Formula Bar** but, this time, use another formula auditing command. Click on the **Show Formulas** command in the **Formula Auditing** group. 4

6. This command allows you to display the formulas in cells, rather than their results, on the sheet. 5 To disable the **Show Formulas** command, use the **Ctrl + `** shortcut.

7. You will now see how you can delete arrows in dependent and precedent cells. Open the **Remove Arrows** command in the **Formula Auditing** group.

8. This command includes the options that allow you to erase the arrows by levels when there is more than one. Click on the **Remove Arrows** option 6 to erase them all from the sheet.

9. The remaining commands included in the **Formula Auditing** group allow you to locate common errors in formulas and to correct them by evaluating each one of their parts. To finish this exercise, save your changes by clicking on the **Save** command in the **Quick Access Toolbar**.

6

You can erase all arrows that indicate dependence or precedence at once or by levels.

3

The **Trace Dependents** command displays arrows that indicate which cells are affected by the value of the selected cell.

5

E	F	
=SUM(B2:D2)	=SUM(B2:C2)	=E2*1
=SUM(B3:D3)	=SUM(B3:C3)	=E3*1
=SUM(B4:D4)	=SUM(B4:C4)	
=SUM(B5:D5)		
=SUM(B6:D6)		
=SUM(B7:D7)		

4

The **Show Formulas** command substitutes the resulting values on the sheet by the original formulas.

Calculating with circular references

A CIRCULAR REFERENCE OCCURS when a formula within a cell refers to that same cell, directly or indirectly. Usually, a circular reference causes an error in Excel; nevertheless, you can deactivate this error and use a circular reference to create an advanced calculation.

1. Select cell **D15** and type **5**. (Change, if necessary, the cell format to **General**.)

2. Select cell **D17**, type **=D15+D17**, and click on the **Enter** button on the **Formula Bar** to confirm the entry.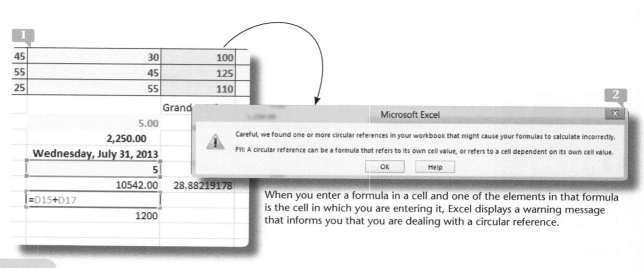

3. A warning message lets you know that you are using a circular reference, that is to say a formula that takes the result as part of the calculation. Click on the **OK** button.

4. The term **Circular References** appears on the **Status Bar**, followed by the name of the cell that contains it. In order to be able to use circular references, you will have to select the appropriate option. Click on the **File** tab, click on the **Options** command, and select the **Formulas** category.

45	30	100
55	45	125
25	55	110

	Grand	
5.00		
2,250.00		
Wednesday, July 31, 2013		
5		
10542.00	28.88219178	
=D15+D17		
1200		

Microsoft Excel

⚠ Careful, we found one or more circular references in your workbook that might cause your formulas to calculate incorrectly.

FYI: A circular reference can be a formula that refers to its own cell value, or refers to a cell dependent on its own cell value.

OK   Help

When you enter a formula in a cell and one of the elements in that formula is the cell in which you are entering it, Excel displays a warning message that informs you that you are dealing with a circular reference.

071

5. Check the **Enable iterative calculation** checkbox in the **Calculation options** area to deactivate the circular calculation errors. ▣

6. Double-click in the **Maximum Iterations** text box, type **1**, and click on the **OK** button to confirm the changes.

7. By allowing iterations and indicating that you only want to perform one iteration per cell, the result of the formula contained in cell **D17** gets updated to value 5. Select cell **D15**, type **6,** and press the **Enter** key to confirm the entry.

8. Observe how the last action has affected cell **D17**. ▣ Value **11** is the result of adding the new contents of cell **D15** to the ones already contained in cell **D17**. Although that works well, you can get unexpected results if you edit the contents of any cell that is not part of the calculation. You will now check that. Select cell **E14**, type **1**, and press **Enter**.

9. Although you have not edited cell **D15**, it has added up again with cell **D17**. ▣ This happened because when you edit a cell, all the formulas in the sheet get calculated again. In order to learn how to solve this problem, you will have to refer to the next practice exercise. For the moment, click on the **Save** button on the **Quick Access Toolbar** to save the changes.

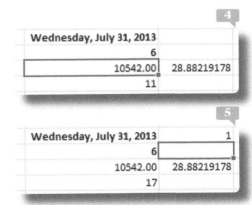

Wednesday, July 31, 2013	
6	
10542.00	28.88219178
11	

Wednesday, July 31, 2013	1
6	
10542.00	28.88219178
17	

Every time you make any changes to the sheet, all the formulas get recalculated and the contents of cell D17 whose formula is **D15+D17** is modified. If you made another change now, the result of cell D17 would be 23 (the result of 17+6).

③

f_x Change options related to formula calculation, performance, and error handling.

Calculation options

Workbook Calculation ⓘ
- ◉ Automatic
- ○ Automatic except for data tables
- ○ Manual
  - ☑ Recalculate workbook before saving

☑ Enable iterative calculation
Maximum Iterations: 100
Maximum Change: 0.001

Working with formulas

- ☐ R1C1 reference style ⓘ
- ☑ Formula AutoComplete ⓘ
- ☑ Use table names in formulas
- ☑ Use GetPivotData functions for PivotTable references

The **Enable iterative calculation** option in the Calculation options category, allows the execution of circular references.

Controlling automatic worksheet recalculation

BY DEFAULT, EXCEL RECALCULATES the whole spreadsheet when changes are made to its cells. This system is very useful and prevents the user from having to force sheet recalculation. Nevertheless, sometimes, when you use circular references or when the system is very slow, you might want the program to wait and do the calculations after you finish editing the worksheet. In this exercise, you will learn how to do this.

1. In the sheet you used for the previous exercise, some of the results were wrong because of the way Excel performs automatic recalculation. In this exercise you will learn how to solve this issue. Click on the **File** tab and click on the **Options** command.

2. Go to the **Formulas** tab in the **Excel Options** box, select **Manual** from the options in the **Calculation options** section, and click on the **OK** button to confirm the change. **1**

3. You will now verify that no automatic recalculations are performed when editing a cell. Select cell **E14**, type **4**, and press **Enter**. **2**

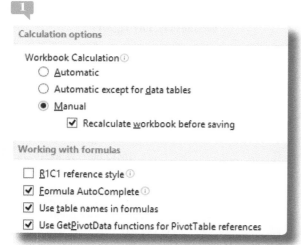

1

Calculation options

Workbook Calculation ⓘ
- ○ Automatic
- ○ Automatic except for data tables
- ◉ Manual
  - ☑ Recalculate workbook before saving

Working with formulas

- ☐ R1C1 reference style ⓘ
- ☑ Formula AutoComplete ⓘ
- ☑ Use table names in formulas
- ☑ Use GetPivotData functions for PivotTable references

On the **Formulas** tab in the **Excel Options** dialog box, select the **Manual** option in order to change the worksheet updates from automatic to manual.

2

	Grand total	840
5.00		
2,250.00		
Wednesday, July 31, 2013	4	
6		
10542.00	28.88219178	
23		
1200		

Notice now that when you change data in the cells, formulas are not automatically updated.

4. Notice that the contents of cell **D17**, where the circular reference is, have not been recalculated. Select cell **D15**, type **-15**, and press **Enter** to confirm the change.

5. There are no changes in cell **D17** because manual calculation is enabled. Select that cell and press the **F9** function key to force the calculation.

6. Try again: Select cell **D15**, enter value **5**, and press the **Enter** key.

7. As it already happened in the previous practice exercise, nothing seems to happen to cell **D17**. Press the **F9** function key to confirm that you want to recalculate the sheet. **3**

8. As you can see, you do not have to select the cell that contains the formula for the recalculation to be performed. If you want to recalculate the formula again, without changing the contents of cell **D15**, all you have to do is use the **F9** key again. Press it to recalculate the formula once more without having to change the contents of cell **D15**.

9. To finish the exercise, select **Automatic** updating again from the **Excel Options** dialog box, **4** and click on the **Save** icon on the **Quick Access Toolbar** to save the changes you made. **5**

072

3

	Grand total	840
5.00		
2,250.00		
Wednesday, July 31, 2013	4	
5		
10542.00	28.88219178	
13		
1200		

If **Manual** data updating is enabled, you will have to press the **F9** function key to execute the action. The cells that contain formulas do not have to be selected in order to be updated when the F9 key is pressed.

4

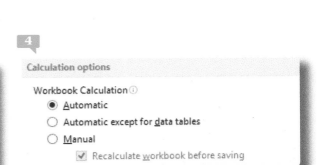

Calculation options

Workbook Calculation ⓘ
- ◉ Automatic
- ○ Automatic except for data tables
- ○ Manual
  - ☑ Recalculate workbook before saving

By default, Excel recalculates the workbook automatically, although, it also has an option that allows you to update all data, except the data in the tables, automatically.

5

FILE | HOME | INSERT | PAGE L

157

Formula auditing

THE WATCH WINDOW COMMAND is another one of the formula auditing tools. It offers full visibility of a formula or formulas in the same spreadsheet. Through this window, the user gets information about the workbook, the sheet, and the cell in which the different formulas are located, and you can even see their syntax and their result.

1. Select cell **E3** in **Sheet1** of the **Points3.xlsx** workbook for instance, which contains a formula.

2. You will begin by opening the so-called **Watch Window** in order to view the information corresponding to the currently selected cell. Click on the **Watch Window** command in the **Formula Auditing** group, on the **Formulas** tab. **1**

3. In order for this window to show information about the formula contained in the selected cell, you have to prompt it to do so. Click on the **Add Watch** button. **2**

4. A new window opens, indicating the reference of the cell you are interested in. Click on the **Add** button in the **Add Watch** dialog box. **3**

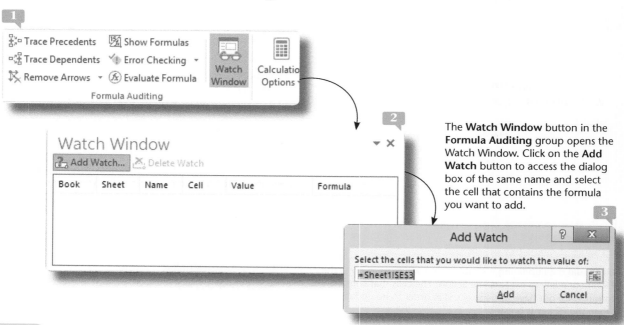

The **Watch Window** button in the **Formula Auditing** group opens the Watch Window. Click on the **Add Watch** button to access the dialog box of the same name and select the cell that contains the formula you want to add.

073

5. The **Watch Window** will automatically show all the information in reference to the selected cell. You will now audit all the formulas in the selected sheet. Go to the **Home** tab, pull down the **Find & Select** command in the **Editing** group, and select the **Go To** option. 🗩

6. Press the **Special** button in the **Go To** dialog box.

7. Select the **Formulas** option in the **Go To Special** dialog box and click on the **OK** button. 🗩

8. Excel selects all the cells in the selected sheet that contain formulas. All you need to do now is to add them to the Watch Window. Click the **Add Watch** button.

9. The **Add Watch** box shows the references of all the selected cells. Click the **Add** button so that all the formulas get added to the **Watch Window**.

10. All the formulas contained in the selected cells are listed in the **Watch Window**. 🗩 This way, any time you want to review the formulas in a spreadsheet that contains a large number of them, you will be able to view them quickly, without having to perform a manual search. To close the **Watch Window** click the **Close** button on its **Title Bar**.

11. Select any cell to deselect all the cells and click on the **Save** button on the **Quick Access Toolbar**.

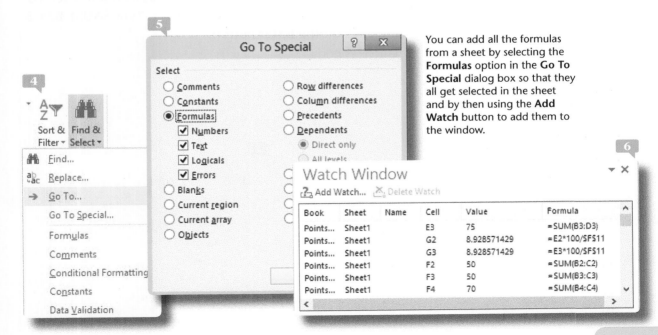

You can add all the formulas from a sheet by selecting the **Formulas** option in the **Go To Special** dialog box so that they all get selected in the sheet and by then using the **Add Watch** button to add them to the window.

Checking errors

THE ERROR CHECKING COMMAND LOCATES and identifies errors that often occur when entering formulas. It also warns the user about what the application detects as possible errors, although in many cases, the user's criteria is what matters and you can often disregard the recommendations.

1. Go to the **Points** table, type **=SUM(B2:C2)** in cell I3, 🔲 and click the **Enter** button.

2. The cell with the formula that you just inserted displays a green triangle in its upper left corner, which marks the existence of a possible error. Click on the **Error Checking** smart tag.

3. An options menu offering options that are related to the error detected in the formula opens. The first option indicates the error found by Excel. In this case the program considers that this formula omits adjacent cells. Imagine that you agree with the program's suggestion and that you decide to modify the formula. Click on the **Update Formula to Include Cells** option. 🔲

4. The formula has been modified as well as its result when you entered cells that it considers incorrect. Type **=SUM(B3:C3)** and click on the **Enter** button.

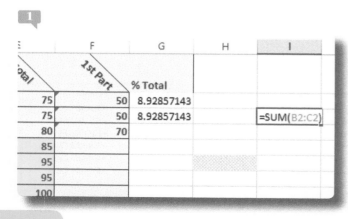

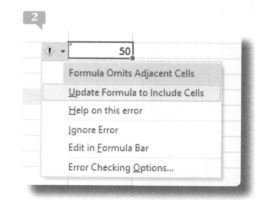

074

5. Click on the **Error Checking** smart tag and this time select the **Help on this error** option.

6. **Excel Help** opens and shows information about how to solve the cell error. To close this window, click on the **X** button in its **Title Bar**.

7. You now decide you want to manually edit the contents of the formula and apply the modifications yourself. Open the Options menu on the smart tag again and select the **Edit in Formula Bar** option.

8. The cell goes into Edit mode in order to let you make the necessary changes. Click the **Enter** button on the **Formula Bar** to leave the formula as it is.

9. If you execute the **Ignore Error** option, the error checking label disappears and the program approves the formula of the selected cell. Click on the smart tag and select the **Ignore Error** option.

10. You will now use the appropriate command to execute error checking. Click on the **Error Checking** command on the **Formulas** tab.

11. The **Error Checking** dialog box opens and shows the same options as the smart tag. To check if there are more cells that contain errors, click the **Next** button, and when you cannot find any more, click **OK**.

Use the **Error Checking** button on the **Formulas** tab to manually check errors in the sheet.

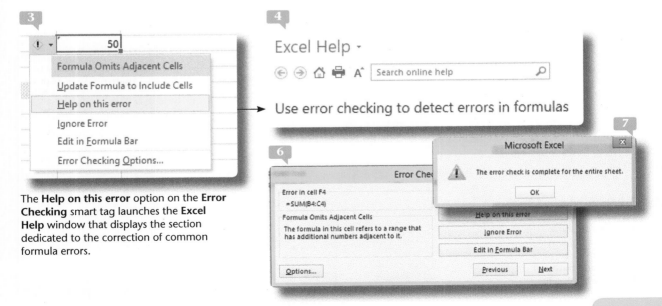

The **Help on this error** option on the **Error Checking** smart tag launches the **Excel Help** window that displays the section dedicated to the correction of common formula errors.

Creating pivot tables

PIVOT TABLE REPORTS GIVE YOU a deep analysis of a data series and offer many different ways to check large databases, calculate subtotals, add numeric data, summarize data by categories and subcategories, filter and sort data sets, and present electronic reports or visually attractive professional brochures. Creating pivot tables with Excel 2013 is easier and more efficient thanks to the new Recommendation and Preview tool.

1. You will continue to use the **Points3** workbook. Select and clear all the cells that do not belong to the table, and make it look like the picture.

2. Select one of the cells in the table, select the **Insert** tab on the **Ribbon,** and click on the **Recommended PivotTable** command.

3. With this new tool, Excel 2013 recommends several ways of summarizing data and offers a preview of each design so that you can pick your favorite. Select the third design in the **Recommended PivotTables** dialog box and click on the **OK** button.

In order to create a pivot table, the data you want to show must have column headers or row headers and must not have any blank cells.

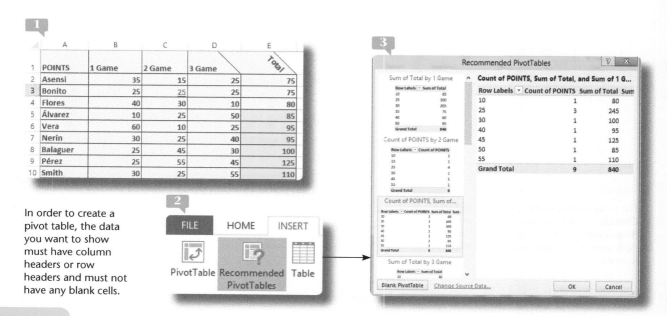

075

4. The pivot table is inserted in a new page of the workbook and the **PivotTable Tools** contextual tab appears. It contains the **Analyze** and **Design** subtabs, which you can use to edit the table. The **PivotTable Fields** task pane opens on the right side of the work area, and this is where you can select the fields that you will show in your report. Check the first field, **Points**, to add it to the report.

5. See the changes to the pivot table, which is now showing the names of the contestants. Deselect the **1Game** field and verify how it affects the table.

6. Thanks to the new function that recommends pivot tables adapted to the data you want to show, choosing a pivot table is now much easier. You can use the traditional function that creates pivot tables from the **Insert** tab or from the **PivotTable Fields** pane by clicking on the **MORE TABLES** button and manually selecting the data you want to show. In order to finish this first exercise dedicated to the creation of pivot tables, click in any cell outside the pivot table to hide the **PivotTable** fields and save your changes.

You can use the arrow button that is next to each field to apply filters so that you can see only the information that interests you.

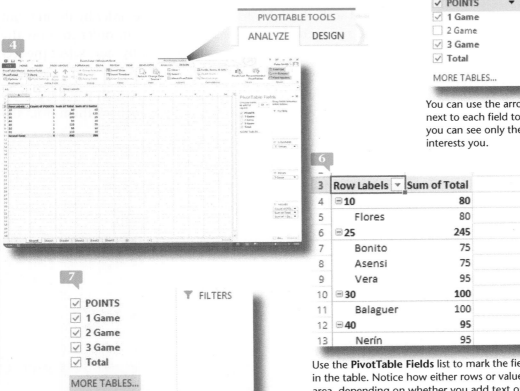

3	Row Labels ▾	Sum of Total
4	⊟10	80
5	Flores	80
6	⊟25	245
7	Bonito	75
8	Asensi	75
9	Vera	95
10	⊟30	100
11	Balaguer	100
12	⊟40	95
13	Nerín	95

Use the **PivotTable Fields** list to mark the fields you want to show in the table. Notice how either rows or values will be added to the area, depending on whether you add text or numbers.

Using field lists to create pivot tables

THE FIELD LIST HAS BEEN UPDATED in this version of Excel to contain pivot tables with one or two tables and makes the search for fields that you might want to show in the tables' layout easier.

1. The **PivotTable Fields** pane should appear automatically when you select any cell in a pivot table. Verify this with the table you created in the previous exercise. ▼**1**

2. If it did not appear, you can launch it by selecting the corresponding option in the **Show** group on the **Analyze** subtab, on the **PivotTable Tools** contextual tab. ▼**2** The **PivotTable Fields** group list has a section where you can select the fields you want to show in your pivot table and another section into which you can drag those fields in order to sort them. You can modify the layout of the sections from the **Tools** button. Click on it.

3. Excel sorts the fields list in **Data Source** order by default, but it lets you change that order to A to Z. In order to show the fields section and the areas section side-by-side, select the second option from the drop-down menu. ▼**3**

4. As you already saw in the previous exercise, all you have to do to add or remove fields is to check or uncheck them from the

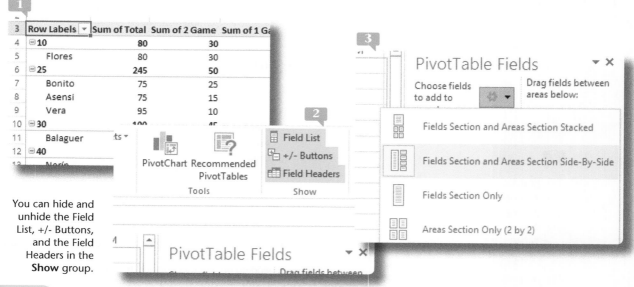

3	Row Labels ▼	Sum of Total	Sum of 2 Game	Sum of 1 Ga
4	⊟10	80	30	
5	Flores	80	30	
6	⊟25	245	50	
7	Bonito	75	25	
8	Asensi	75	15	
9	Vera	95	10	
10	⊟30	100	45	
11	Balaguer			
12	⊟40			
13	Nerín			

You can hide and unhide the Field List, +/- Buttons, and the Field Headers in the **Show** group.

PivotChart Recommended PivotTables

Tools

⊞ Field List
⊞ +/- Buttons
⊞ Field Headers

Show

PivotTable Fields ▼ ✕

Choose fields to add to

Drag fields between areas below:

Fields Section and Areas Section Stacked

Fields Section and Areas Section Side-By-Side

Fields Section Only

Areas Section Only (2 by 2)

PivotTable Fields ▼ ✕

076

list. Usually, nonnumeric fields are added to the **Rows** area, numeric fields are added to the **Values** area, and **Online Analytical Processing** date and time hierarchies are added to the **Columns** area. Check the **1 Game** field check box to select it.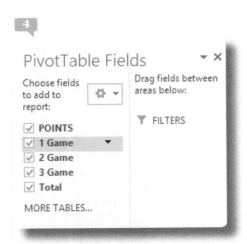

5. You will notice that a new column is added to the pivot table. **Columns** area fields are shown as **Column Labels** at the top of the pivot table; **Rows** area fields are shown as **Row Labels** on the left side of the table, and **Values area** fields are shown as summarized numeric values. As mentioned previously, you can drag fields in order to change the way they are shown in the table. As an example, you will move the **Sum of 1 Game** that you just added. Click on the bottom part of the list of values scroll bar, click on the last value that corresponds to the column you are dealing with, and drag it until it is in the first position.

6. Every field has its own settings box that you can access both from its menu in the **Pivot Table Fields** pane and from the **Analyze** subtab. Click the **Field Settings** button in the **Active Field** group.

7. This launches the **Field Settings** dialog box in which you can type a custom name for the field, select the type of calculation you want to use to summarize the data and the way you want to show the values. To finish the exercise, get out of this box by clicking the **Cancel** button and save the changes you made to the sheet.

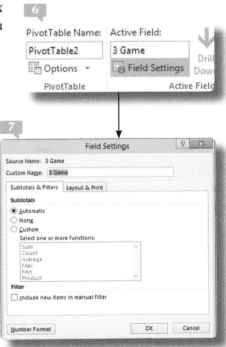

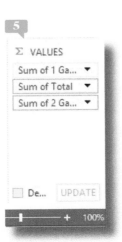

Creating a data model

ANOTHER INTERESTING NEW FEATURE in Excel 2013 regarding pivot tables is that you can create pivot tables that are based on several tables, whereas you could only do that before if you had PowerPivot. In this version, you can import different tables and create relationships between them in order to analyze their data.

1. A data model is the new method offered by Excel 2013 to integrate data from multiple tables and build a relational data source. In this exercise, you will learn how to use this new function and for that purpose, you will use the **Childrens Books** database that you already used in a previous exercise and that can be found on our website. Select a free cell in the current sheet, select the **Data** tab, and click on the **From Access** button in the **Get External Data** group.

2. In the **Select Data Source** dialog box, locate and select the **Childrens Books** database, and click on the **Open** button.

3. The **Select Table** dialog box shows all the tables that are stored in your sample database. Select the **Enable selection of multiple tables** option, select the **Price+VAT** and **Childrens Books** tables, and click the **OK** button.

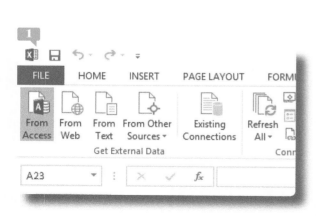

077

4. The **Import Data** dialog box opens, in which you have to indicate how you want to view the data in your workbook and where you want to place it. The visualization options that allow you to work with the whole set of tables are: **PivotTable Report**, **PivotChart**, and **Power View Report**. In this example, keep the **PivotTable Report** option selected, select the **New worksheet** option, and click on the **OK** button.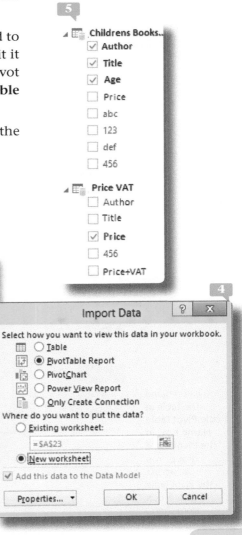

5. Look at the result. A new page of the workbook now shows the tools you need to create a pivot table whose data source will be the two Access tables you selected. You now need to select what fields from those tables you want to add to the report. Select the **Author**, **Title**, and **Age** fields from the **Childrens Books** table and the **Price** field in the **Price VAT** table from the **Pivot**Table Fields task pane.

6. You can then see how the fields from both tables get added to the pivot table report. Once the report is built, you can edit it manually from the **Analyze** and **Design** subtabs of the pivot table, as you will see in the next exercise. Hide the **PivotTable Fields** panel by clicking the **X** button on its header.

7. Click the **Save** icon on the **Quick Access Toolbar** to save the changes you made to the workbook.

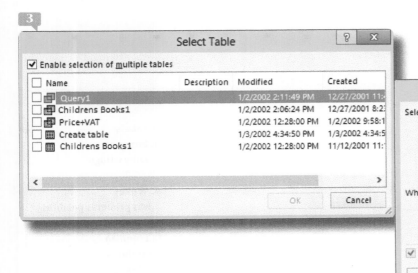

Editing pivot tables

IMPORTANT

The commands that allow you to clear data from a table, select it, or move the table to another location can be found in the **Actions** group, on the **Analyze** subtab, in the PivotTable tools.

A PIVOT TABLE IS LINKED TO ITS DATA source table or tables, and that data can be updated either manually or automatically, depending on the settings. Excel also allows you to quickly apply a preset style to a pivot table or chart.

1. When you are creating a pivot table and it is selected, the **Pivot Table Tools** contextual tab, which includes the **Analyze** and **Design** subtabs, appears. The tools included on this tab allow you to modify the aspect of the pivot table. You will now see what name Excel assigns pivot tables by default. As you can see, in the **Analyze** subtab, you can edit the name of the table, which is **PivotTable1**, from here and access its different options. 🔳

2. Click the arrow button in the **Row Labels** field, in the pivot table. 🔳

3. This button allows you to sort the fields and apply filters. Imagine you just want to show the names of some authors in the table. Check the **Select All** check box and then select the ones you want to show, and click **OK**. 🔳

You can rename the table in the **PivotTable Name** box, in the **PivotTable** group. You can access the PivotTable Options box from there.

Click the arrow button of the **Row Labels** field to see the available options.

4. The small icon that appears on the right of the **Row Labels** shows that you have applied a filter.  You will now apply a new, more eye-catching style to the table. Click on the **Design** subtab.

5. Click on the **More** button, which is the third arrow in the **PivotTable Styles** group, to see other available styles.

6. Select the third style in the **Medium** group from the PivotTables Quick Styles gallery, 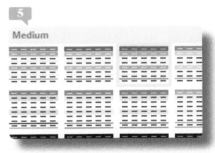 for instance, and see the result.

7. Besides changing the style of the table, you can modify the value fields titles, sort data, etc. Go to the **PivotTable Options** dialog box to see what other settings are available in Excel. Go to the **Analyze** subtab again.

8. Click on the **Options** command in the **PivotTable** group.

9. The **PivotTable Options** dialog box appears and you can define its design and its format, hide or unhide totals and other elements, add filters, determine how the table will print, and set options related to the data it contains. Click on the **Printing** tab.

10. Select the **Set print titles** option and click on the **OK** button.

11. Click in any blank cell to deselect the table and use the **Save** command on the **Quick Access Toolbar** to save the changes.

Apply one of the styles you will find in the **Quick Styles gallery** to your pivot table.

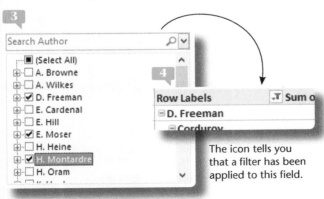

Use the header filters to hide and unhide data in your table.

The icon tells you that a filter has been applied to this field.

Importing data from Windows Azure DataMarket

EXCEL 2013 LETS YOU USE MULTIPLE tables in the Excel data model. For that purpose, you can connect to data and also import it from external sources such as OData, Windows Azure Datamarket, or SharePoint, which offer free data.

1. In this exercise, dedicated to downloading data from Windows azure Datamarket, you will learn how to show the **PowerPivot** tab on the Excel **Ribbon**. Open a new blank workbook, click on the **File** tab, and click on **Options**.

2. Select the **Customize Ribbon** category from the **Excel Options** dialog box.

3. Select POWERPIVOT from the Main Tabs list and click **OK** so that it will appear on the **Ribbon**. 📝

4. With Excel 2013, you can use this add-in to create fancy Data models. Select the **PowerPivot** tab and click on the **Manage** button in the **Data Model** group. 📝

5. The **PowerPivot for Excel** window appears now and it displays the workbook that you created at the beginning of the exercise. In order to access the Windows Azure DataMarket data service, click on the **From Data Service** button in the **Get External Data** group and select the **From Windows Azure Marketplace** option. 📝

The tab for the **PowerPivot** add-ons is in the Main Tabs category, on the Customize tab, on the Ribbon.

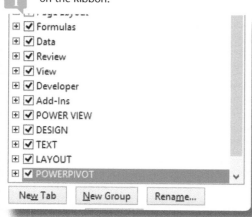

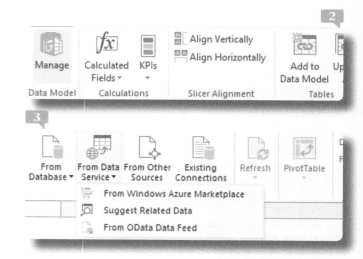

6. The **Table Import Wizard** opens, and you are offered a large catalog of resources  that may be from free data providers or from providers that charge for the data or only offer a free trial. You can use the search engine to locate specific data or filter the results by selecting options from the left pane. Click on the **Free** link in the **Price** section and then on the **Science and statistics** category.

7. Browse the results list and click on the **Subscribe** button for the **DateStream** table, for example.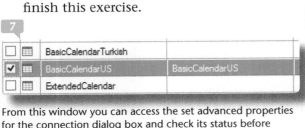

8. In order to be able to use resources from this data source, you must have a Microsoft account and enter the account log-in information on this screen. Type your e-mail address and your password in the corresponding text boxes and click on the **Log in** button.

9. Once you have logged in to the service, you will be shown a preview of the table you have chosen. Click on the **Unlimited Transactions Free** button and the **Sign Up** button.

10. In the next window, click on the **Continue** button and the **Select Query** button. In the **Table Import Wizard** window that shows the descriptive name connection, click the **Next** button.

11. You will import the data from the **BasicCalendarUS** source table. Select it and click on the **Finish** button.

12. The length of the import process will depend on the amount of data contained in the table you have selected. Once the process is over, Excel will inform you of the amount of transferred files. Click on the **X** to close the wizard and save the PowerPivot workbook in your document library in order to finish this exercise.

079

> ## IMPORTANT
>
> It is possible to build a relational data source among tables from different sources, in order to simplify the analysis of the data without having to consolidate it all in just one table.

The way **Window Azure DataMarket** is organized makes external data accessible.

7

☐	BasicCalendarTurkish	
☑	BasicCalendarUS	BasicCalendarUS
☐	ExtendedCalendar	

From this window you can access the set advanced properties for the connection dialog box and check its status before proceeding to download the data.

DateStream
Boyan Penev
Date table feed designed for import into an Excel PowerPivot model. The table contains columns particularly suitable for time business intelligence applications. Delivered through the Azure Data Market, it is effortlessly available through the PowerPivot window in Excel.

Creating relationships between tables

IN ORDER TO SIMPLIFY DATA ANALYSIS between tables with data sources from different tables, Excel now offers the possibility to create relationships between tables, which avoids having to consolidate that data into another table. In this exercise, you will see a practical example based on two tables downloaded from Windows Azure DataMarket.

1. Following the steps you learned in the previous exercise, download another data table from Windows Azure DataMarket, more specifically, the one called **US AIR Carrier Flight Delays**, and insert it in a new sheet in the workbook. (Remember that the process can take several minutes depending on the amount of data you are importing.) In order to create a data model relationship between this table and the one you imported in the previous exercise, they need to have compatible columns. Notice that the format of the **DateKey** column in the **BasicCalendarUS** 🟦 and the **FlightDate** column from the **US AIR Carrier Flight** table are the same. 🟦 You will use those columns to create a relationship between both tables. Click on the **PivotTable** button in the **PowerPivot for Excel** window. 🟦

2. Keep the **New Worksheet** option selected in the **Insert Pivot** dialog box and click the **OK** button. 🟦

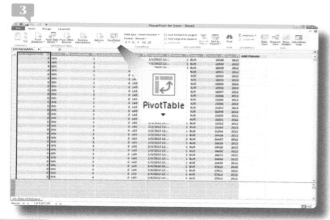

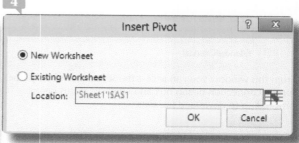

If you want to insert the pivot table into an existing spreadsheet, check this option in the **Insert Pivot** dialog box and, if necessary, collapse it to select the cell in which the table will be located in the sheet.

080

3. As indicated, you now have to select the fields that you want to add to the report. Expand the fields of the **On Time Performance** table in the **PivotTable Fields** task pane and select the **ArrDelayMinutes** option so that it is added to the values area. 5

4. The total amount of minutes that the flights were delayed will appear in the pivot table. Show the **BasicCalendarUS** table fields and check **MonthInCalendar** to add it to the row area. 6

5. There are some identical values that need a relationship to be created between the tables, just as it tells you on the **Create** button that has just appeared in the fields box. Click on it.

6. This action will launch the **Create Relationship** dialog box that you will use to create the relationship. Select **BasicCalendarUS** in the **Table** field and select **Datekey** in the **Column (Foreign)** field.

7. Select the **On Time Performance** table in the **Related Table** field and select **FlightDate** in the **Related Column (Primary)** field. 7

8. Click the **OK** button and notice that the sum of delayed minutes now is different for every month. 8

9. To organize the pivot table better, expand the fields of the **BasicCalendarUS** table in the Fields pane and then drag the **Yearkey** field and drop it on the **MonthInCalendar** field, in the row area. See the result in the table 9 and save the changes you made to the sheet.

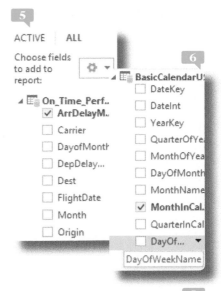

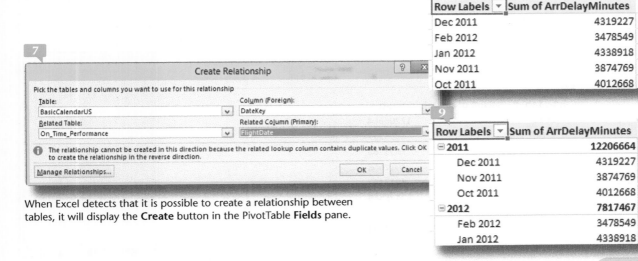

When Excel detects that it is possible to create a relationship between tables, it will display the **Create** button in the PivotTable **Fields** pane.

Drilling into pivot table data

IN EXCEL 2013 YOU CAN USE the new Data tracking options to navigate more easily to different levels of detail in a data model. Exploring data in a complex pivot table can be time-consuming; in Excel 2013, the new Quick Explore feature makes this task easier.

1. In this exercise, you will keep on working with the pivot table you created in the previous exercises, using sources you imported from Windows Azure DataMarket. Select the cell that contains the year **2011** label and click on the new **Quick Explore** button that appears in the lower right corner. 🛑

2. You have to select the elements you want to explore in the **Explore** box that appears. Expand the **BasicCalendarUS** table fields, select, for example, the **Datekey** field, and click on the **Drill To DateKey** button. 🛑

3. Notice now that the data is expanded on the table. You must remember that the way data can be explored in a pivot table depends on its hierarchy. Logically, in order to make the most of this new tool, the table should have data on multiple levels. You will next make sure your sample table does not have any more sublevels to explore, and you will see how Excel behaves when trying to use the new **Quick Explore**

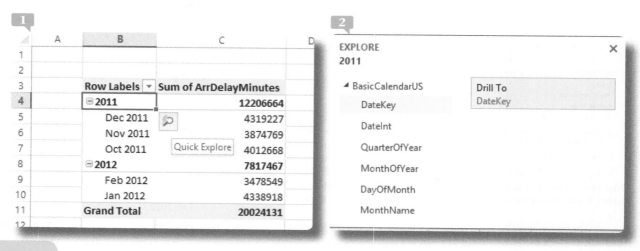

174

function. Click on any cell in the pivot table and click on the **Quick Explore** icon.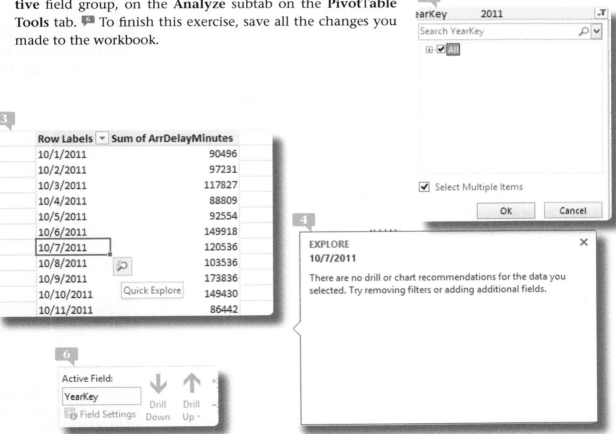

081

4. Back to the **Explore** box, the program informs you that there are no recommended charts or further exploring for the related data, which does not have a subcategory. It advises you to try and remove the filters or to add more fields to the tables in order to be able to use the Explore function. Close the **Explore** box by clicking on the **X** in the title area.

5. In order to remove the Explore filter you have used, click on the icon that appears in the cell that shows the year 2011, select the **All** checkbox in the pop-up window, and click on the **OK** button.

6. When you practice on your own with tables that have more hierarchy levels, you will see that the Drill tool offers two options: Drill Down and drill Up. You will have to use them as needed, and pick the level you want to drill to. You can find both options on the **Quick Explore** icon and also in the **Active** field group, on the **Analyze** subtab on the **Pivot**Table **Tools** tab. To finish this exercise, save all the changes you made to the workbook.

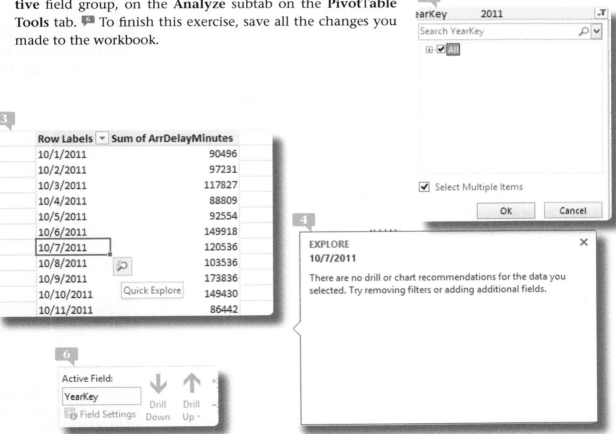

Creating pivot charts

A PIVOT CHART IS A GRAPHICAL REPRESENTATION of the data in a PivotTable report, although it can also be created from worksheet data. In those cases, an associated PivotTable report is created automatically. A pivot chart is interactive, so the data can be sorted and filtered in order to show the underlying data.

1. In this exercise, you will create a pivot chart on Sheet6 of your **Points3.xlsx** sample workbook, from a pivot table that you created earlier. Select the pivot table and select the **Analyze** subtab on the **PivotTable Tools** contextual tab.

2. Click on the **PivotChart** command in the **Tools** group. 📮1

3. The **Insert Chart** dialog box opens and you can use it to select the type of chart you will insert. Select the fourth model of the **Column** type and click **OK**. 📮2

4. The new chart is inserted in the middle of the page. If you applied a filter to the table, you will notice that the chart has kept it and shows the appropriate results. Uncheck **Total** in the **PivotTable Fields** list, for example. 📮3

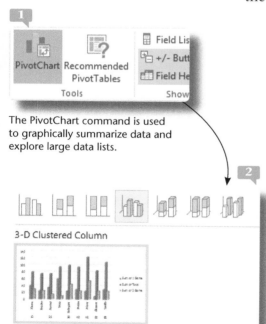

The PivotChart command is used to graphically summarize data and explore large data lists.

3-D Clustered Column

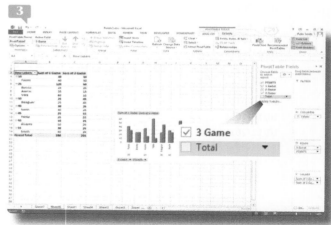

A pivot chart is created from pivot table data and if the latter has a filter applied to it, that filter will also be applied to the chart.

5. The field disappears both from the table and from the pivot chart. You will now see how to create a chart from worksheet data. Go back to the sheet where the main **Points** table is located.

6. Select the **Insert** tab, go to the **Charts** group, click on the arrow button of the **PivotChart** tool, and select the **PivotChart & PivotTable** option.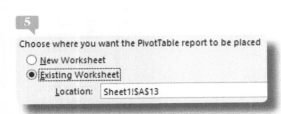

7. The **Create Pivot Table** dialog box opens and there you can select the range of cells you want to include in the chart. The process is the same as the one you used to create a pivot table. In the **Table/Range** field, use the **Shift** key to select cells **A2:E10**.

8. In the **Location** box, select the **Existing Worksheet** option and click in a blank cell on the current sheet.

9. Press the **OK** button to create the table and the chart.

10. At the indicated spot, a table and a blank pivot chart are inserted and **PivotChart Fields** pane is enabled. Select all the fields and notice how they are added both to the pivot chart and to the table.

11. Click in an empty cell in the sheet to deselect the pivot table and use the **Save** command from the **Quick Access Toolbar** to save the changes.

082

IMPORTANT

In Excel 2013 an animated chart does not have to be associated to a pivot table, it can be independent and allow you to navigate to data details thanks to the **Drill Down** and **Drill Up** tools.

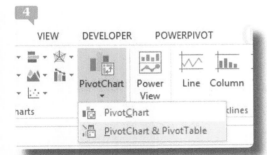

The **PivotChart** option on the **Insert** tab allows you to create pivot charts from worksheet data.

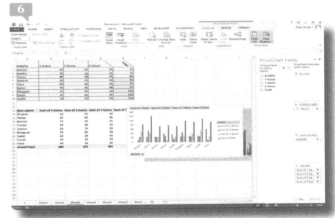

Pivot charts can be modified once created. You can apply filters to them to help you analyze the information you need.

Creating slicers

SINCE EXCEL 2010, YOU CAN FILTER DATA with slicers that provide buttons you can click on, to filter data in pivot tables. Slicers, which have been improved in Excel 2013, also indicate the current filtering state, which makes it easier to understand what exactly is shown in a filtered PivotTable report.

1. You will create a slicer on the pivot table you have already created. Click on the pivot table in order to launch the **Pivot-Table Tools** contextual tab.

2. Click on **Insert Slicer** in the **Filter** group on the **Analyze** subtab.

3. This opens the **Insert Slicers** dialog box. In this dialog box you must select the table fields for which you want to create a slicer. In this case, select the first one and click on the **OK** button. **2**

4. This will create a slicer that will be placed next to the pivot table. Click on the slicer and hold the mouse button down to drag the slicer to a spot where it does not get in your way. **3**

5. In Excel 2013, slicers are easier to use and set up, and they show the current filter so that you can know exactly what data

The **Insert Slicer** command on the **PivotTable Tools** contextual tab allows you to create slicers that will speed up the application of filters.

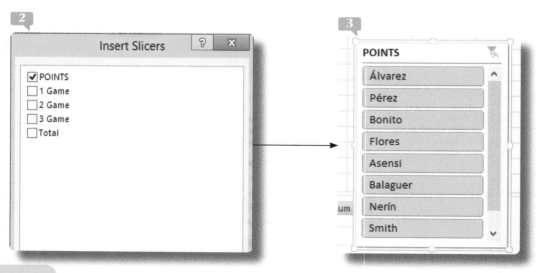

Each field will create an independent slicer. You can create as many slicers as there are data fields.

083

you are analyzing. Imagine that you are only interested in one of the players' results. Go to the slicer and click on the first player to select him. 🗨

6. Look at the result. The rest of the players have been automatically deselected and both the pivot table and the pivot chart show the results of the player you selected. Notice as well that the Filter icon is now enabled. Click on it to undo the selection and thus remove the filter. 🗨

7. All the fields appear again and the filter icon is disabled. Those filters that are applied just by selecting the elements you want to view allow you to select one or several elements. You will now try to show the results for three of the players. Click on the first player.

8. Press on the **Ctrl** key, click on the third player, and then on the last one. 🗨

9. Before finishing, you will disable the filter. This time, click on the first field in the slicer and click on the last field while holding down the **Shift** key, in order to select all the players and remove the filter.

10. Click on the slicer and press the **Del** key on your keyboard to remove it.

You can use the **Ctrl** key to select nonconsecutive fields.

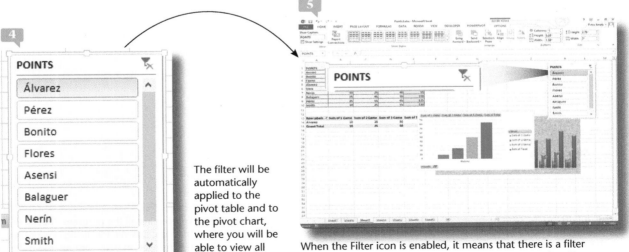

The filter will be automatically applied to the pivot table and to the pivot chart, where you will be able to view all the selected fields.

When the Filter icon is enabled, it means that there is a filter selected. If you click on that icon you will eliminate that filter.

Inserting a Power View Report (I)

OFFICE PROFESSIONAL PLUS COMES with the Power View feature that allows you to create charts and interact with them, and also to create slicers and other data visualization. The Advanced View option in Excel 2013, to which the Power View feature corresponds, can be enabled from the Insert tab, but you need to install the Silverlight add-in in order to use it.

1. In this first exercise dedicated to the **Power View** feature in Excel 2013, you will see what your **Sheet1** from the **Points3.xlsx** sample table looks like in Power View. This feature of the program makes data visualization and exploration easier. Select the cells that make up the data table for **Sheet1**, select the **Insert** tab, and click on the **Power View** button in the **Reports** group. 🗨

2. The first time you access Power View, Excel asks you to install the **Silverlight** add-in. Click on the **Install Silverlight** hyperlink in the Message Bar that appears on top of the sheet. 🗨

3. Click the **Run** button in the download progress window 🗨 and click the **Install Now** button in the **Installation** window.

4. Once the installation is over, click the **Close** button on this window and on the Downloads window and click the **Reload** button on the Message Bar.

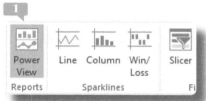

Microsoft Silverlight is an add-in that allows you to develop enhanced applications for the Internet. You need this add-in to be able to work with Power View.

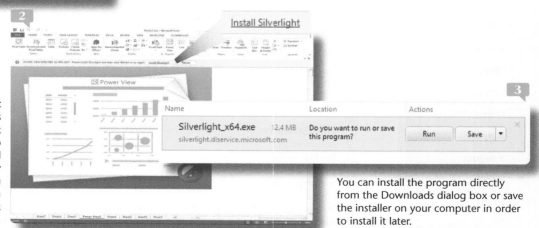

You can install the program directly from the Downloads dialog box or save the installer on your computer in order to install it later.

180

5. Notice that a new sheet called **Power View** has been added to the workbook and that there is now a new tab on the **Ribbon** with tools that will allow you to edit the appearance of the data you want to show. Go to the **Power View Fields** pane and select the fields you want to show in the report. Expand the fields of the **Range** table. 4

6. Select all the fields in this table and notice how they show both in the fields area and in the report. 5

7. Just as when working with pivot tables, **Power View** also allows you to modify the order in which the fields are shown in the report. Drag the **POINTS** field in the **FIELDS** area to first place and notice how the report changes. 6

8. You will now add a filter to the report, which will make data analysis easier. Drag and drop the **1 Game** field from the fields list to the **Filters** section of the report. 7

9. If you click on the **List filter mode** icon, which is the first icon on the right in the field that has been added to the **Filters** pane, you will see several filtering systems, such as the one that lets you show elements that match certain criteria. Check that this is the case. 8

10. To show certain values in the table from which you have taken the data, you can also enable **TABLE VIEW** on the filters pane or use the Filter icon that appears on the table in the report when you select the table. In the next exercise, you will keep on practicing with the Power View editing options. To finish this exercise, deselect the report and save the changes you made to the workbook.

6

FIELDS

POINTS	▼
Σ 1 Game	▼
Σ 3 Game	▼
Σ 2 Game	▼
Σ Total	▼

7

Filters   ‹ ✕

VIEW | TABLE

◢ 1 Game   ⇥ ✎ ✕
(All)

10   60

8

Filters   ‹ ✕

VIEW | TABLE

◢ 1 Game   ⇥ ✎ ✕
(All)

Show items for which the value:

is greater than or equal to   ▼

And   Or

apply filter

4

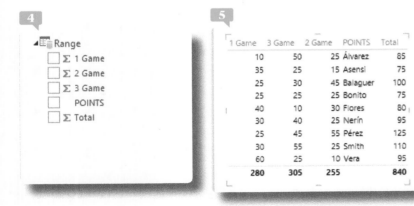

◢ ⊞ Range
☐ Σ 1 Game
☐ Σ 2 Game
☐ Σ 3 Game
☐   POINTS
☐ Σ Total

5

1 Game	3 Game	2 Game	POINTS	Total
10	50	25	Álvarez	85
35	25	15	Asensi	75
25	30	45	Balaguer	100
25	25	25	Bonito	75
40	10	30	Flores	80
30	40	25	Nerín	95
25	45	55	Pérez	125
30	55	25	Smith	110
60	25	10	Vera	95
280	305	255		840

Inserting a Power View Report (II)

WHEN YOU CREATE A POWER VIEW REPORT, Excel allows you to edit its appearance with the Power View tab tools. Besides being able to change the way data is presented in the report (as a chart, as a table, as a map, etc.), you can customize the appearance of the report by applying a specific theme, adding a background image, inserting your own photographs, etc.

1. In this exercise, you will keep practicing with the Power View tool for Excel 2013. You will learn how to modify the appearance of the simple report you created in the previous exercise by taking the data from the table in the **Points3.xlsx** sample workbook. You will begin by adding a title to the report. Click on the placeholder text: **Click here to add a title**. 🗨 Type **Points Report** 🗨 and click out of the text box to confirm the entry.

2. You will now apply a preset Office theme to your report. Remember that themes are combinations of colors and fonts that allow you to easily modify the appearance of a report. Click on the **Themes** button in the group of the same name on the **Power View** tab and select, for instance, the second theme in the fourth row, called **Austin**. 🗨

3. Notice how both the colors and the fonts change in the report and also in the list of filters. In order to apply a background you can select one of the preset backgrounds for the

Click here to add a title

Points Report

You can easily change the title text characteristics with the usual tools on the **Home** tab.

selected theme and also add your own image that is stored on your computer. You will learn how to do both. Press the Background button in the Themes group and choose one of the availables themes. 4

4. On this preset background, you will add your own image. Click on the **Set Image** button in the **Background Image** group and click on **Set Image**. 5

5. This will launch the **Open** dialog box in which you have to find the image you want to use as a background for your report. Choose an image that is saved on your computer and click on the **Open** button. 6

6. See how the appearance of the report starts changing (and improving). With the rest of the commands in the **Background Image** group, you can modify the position of the image in the report and its degree of transparency. Click on the **Transparency** button and select **70%** as a value. 7

7. Using the **View Group** options, you can hide and unhide the Fields list and the Filters area and you can also show the report in its real size rather than fitting it in the window. You will finish the exercise by changing the pivot table view mode in the report. Select the **Design** tab.

8. Click on the **Tiles** button in the group of the same name so that the data is represented as a series of tiles. 8

9. The appearance of the data changes. Click on the arrow button to move around the table and you will see the values that correspond to the player **Smith**, for example. 9

10. To finish the exercise, click on the **Save** icon on the **Quick Access Toolbar** to save the changes you made to the workbook.

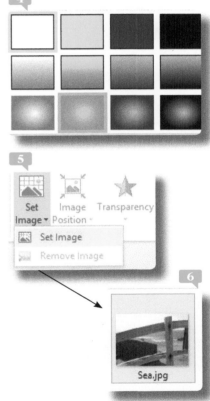

Sea.jpg

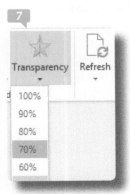

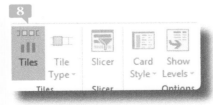

The Tiles data display has two options, Tab Strip and Tile Flow that can be applied from the **Tile Type** button.

Creating and running a macro

MACROS ARE AN EASY WAY to program a series of orders. When you select the Record a Macro function, all the actions from that point until the end of the recording are saved for future use.

1. The tools for creating and running macros can be found on the **Developer** tab, which is hidden by default. Select **Sheet1** in the **Points3.xlsx** workbook, go to the **Excel Options** dialog box from the **File** tab, select the **Developer** option in the **Customize Ribbon** category, and click on the **OK** button. **1**

2. Select the **Developer** tab and click the **Record Macro** command in the **Code** group. **2**

3. In the **Record Macro** dialog box, keep the default name given by Excel to the new macro, **Macro1**, and in the **Shortcut key** text box, type **q**. **3**

4. You can indicate where you are going to save the macro, which will be this same workbook by default, and add a brief description. Click the **OK** button.

By default, the **Developer** tab is hidden in Excel. To show it you must enable the appropriate option in the **Customize Options Ribbon** category in the Program Option box.

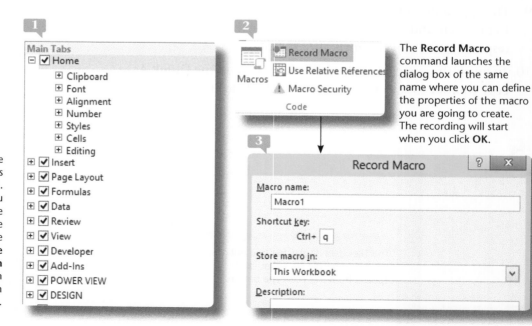

The **Record Macro** command launches the dialog box of the same name where you can define the properties of the macro you are going to create. The recording will start when you click **OK**.

5. All your actions from this point on will be recorded on the macro, therefore, it is essential not to make mistakes. Notice that there is now a button with a square on it on the Status Bar; This is the **Stop recording** button. Click and hold down the **Alt** key and type **126** in an empty cell and click **Enter**. (This combination gives you the ~ symbol).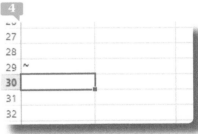

6. Use the button that appeared on the **Status Bar** or the **Stop Recording** command in the **Code** group to stop recording the macro.

7. To run the macro by using a shortcut, click in an empty cell and press the **Ctrl+Q** shortcut keys.

8. You will now run the macro again by using a different system. Click in an empty cell and click the **Macros** button in the **Code** group to access the **Macro** dialog box.

9. Make sure that the only macro, **Macro1**, that you have created until now is selected in the dialog box and click the **Run** button.

10. In order to finish this exercise, you will delete the macro. Click the **Macros** button to go back to the **Macro** dialog box.

11. From this window, you can show all the steps that make up the selected macro, you can edit it, delete it, or display its Options box. Keep **Macro1** selected and click on the **Delete** button.

12. Click **Yes** in the dialog box that appears to confirm that you want to delete the macro.

The **Alt + 126** shortcut in Excel gives you the ~ symbol.

You can stop the recoding with the **Stop Recording** button in the **Code** group or in the same button on the **Status Bar**.

The **Macros** button opens the **Macro** dialog box, which allows you to record, run, edit, delete, and choose options for macros.

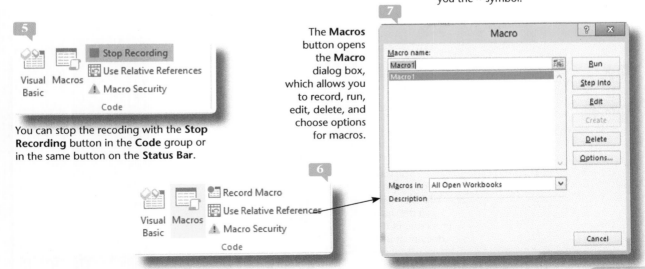

Getting a live preview

THE SIZE OF THE SCREEN does not usually match the size of the paper on which the documents are going to be printed, and it can be hard to know what part of the spreadsheet will fit the paper you had planned to use how the document will split when you spread it over several sheets of paper. Excel 2013 comes with the **Print** command on the **File** tab that directly lets you get a live preview of the part of the sheet that you are going to print.

1. Excel 2010 has made previewing a document a lot easier. In this exercise, you will learn the different ways you can preview your spreadsheets before printing them. You will continue practicing with the **Points3.xlsx** sample book. Click on the **File** tab. 🔲

2. Remember that some of the options on this tab are new to this version of the program. In its right pane, the **Information** command displays a list of the open workbook's properties. Click on the **Print** command. 🔲

3. The **Print** command then shows you a live preview of the selected sheet's print area on the right of the pane. 🔲 Click on the round arrow button in the **File** menu to go back to your worksheet.

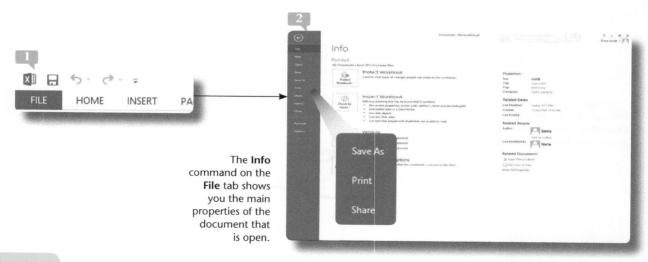

The **Info** command on the **File** tab shows you the main properties of the document that is open.

087

4. When you enable Live Preview, the program marks the print area of the sheet with a dotted marquee. You will now learn another way of getting a live preview for the sheet. Select the **Page Layout** tab on the **Ribbon**.

5. In the **Page Setup** group, you will find all the commands that will allow you to adjust the page in order to obtain the desired printing. Almost all the commands in this group are the ones that you can find in the **Print** command on the **File** tab. Click on the **Page Setup** group dialog launcher. 4

6. This launches the **Page Setup** dialog box for printing. 5 In this box, click on the **Print Preview** button and see what happens.

7. The **Print** command on the **File** tab loads again and shows a live preview of the document, on the right. In the next exercise you will learn how to adjust the settings for all the elements of the sheet that play a part in the printing process. To finish this exercise, click on the round arrow button on the **File** tab to get out of the live preview.

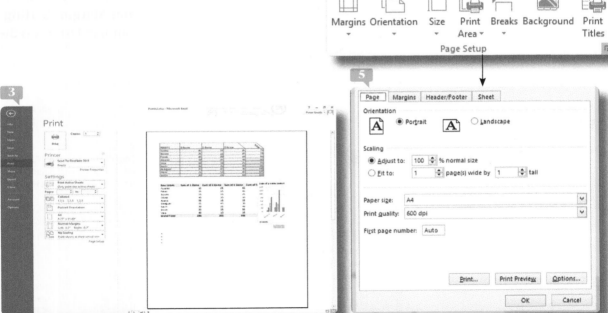

The **Print** command on the **File** tab automatically shows a live preview of the document.

The **Print Preview** of the **Page Setup** dialog box launches the **Print** section on the **File** tab.

Setting up a page for printing

FROM THE FILE TAB, YOU CAN SET the different parameters for your printing and access the complete Page Settings dialog box. The Tools group in the Page Layout tab on the Options Ribbon allows you to set a number of parameters including page orientation, margins, the size of the paper, columns, page breaks, line numbers, and hyphens. You can also access the Page Setup dialog box from this tab.

1. Select the **File** tab and click on the **Print** command.

2. This allows you to access the main commands related to pre-printing and printing. You will now change the page orientation. Pull down the text box that says **Portrait Orientation** and select **Landscape Orientation**. 🔲

3. The program offers a number of predefined margin settings that can be modified. Click on the first of the two icons on the lower right part of the Live Preview pane to show the margins. 🔲

4. You can modify the margins on the preview or by assigning specific values. Pull down the **Last Custom Margins Settings** field and click on the **Custom Margins** command to access the **Page Setup** dialog box. 🔲

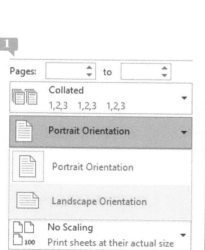

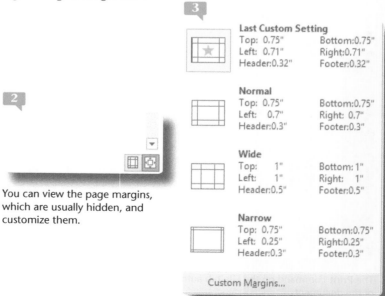

You can view the page margins, which are usually hidden, and customize them.

5. The dialog box opens directly on the contents of the **Margins** tab. Check the **Horizontally** checkbox in the **Center** on **page** section.

6. You can see the result in the small preview within the dialog box. Select the **Vertically** option and click **OK** to go back to the menu with a live preview.

7. Another way you can access the Settings dialog box is through the **Page Setup** link. Click on that link which is located below the Scale command.

8. Click on the **Sheet** tab in the **Page Setup** dialog box.

9. On this tab you can set a specific print area: select only one cell range to print. Check the **Gridlines** option in the **Print** section, and click the **OK** button.

10. The **Print** command button allows you to start printing once the settings for the page are complete, if you have a printer installed on your system. Double-click the top arrowhead button in the **Copies** field to set **3** as the number of copies you want printed.

11. To finish this exercise, click on the **Print** button to print the document.

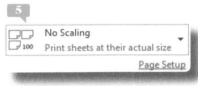

The **Page settings** link launches the dialog box of the same name in which you can establish settings for the page and adjust it correctly before printing.

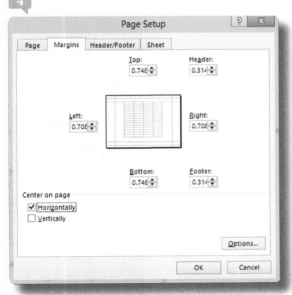

The contents of this page can be centered both horizontally and vertically.

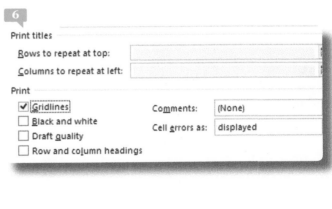

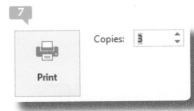

The book will be sent to the device that has been selected in the **Printer** field.

Working in Page Layout View

PAGE LAYOUT VIEW IS SIMILAR TO PREVIEW. It is a view that allows the user to adjust the page and prepare it for printing.

1. In this exercise, you will learn how to use the **Page Layout View.** You can access the Page Layout View from the appropriate icon on the **Status Bar** or from the corresponding command on the **View** tab. Select this tab on the **Ribbon**.

2. Click on the **Page Layout** command in the **Workbook Views** group.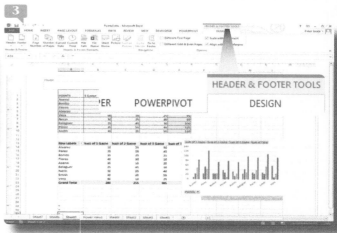

3. Another view icon appears in the **Status Bar.** From this view you create up the header and edit the page margins with the help of horizontal and vertical rulers. You will now change the header. Click on the **Click to add header** phrase.

4. The header is now shown in editing mode and the **Header & Footer Tools** contextual tab appears. Type **1** and click on cell **A2** to confirm the entry.

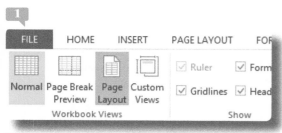

When you select the header in order to edit it, the **Header & Footer Tools** contextual tab is automatically enabled.

Use the icons from the **Workbook Views** group on the **View** tab or the visualization icons on the **Status Bar** to get different views.

089

5. White spaces appear around the cells to indicate the sheet margins. These spaces can be hidden and unhidden with a simple click on any sheet border. 4️⃣

6. You can drag the rulers shown in this view to modify the page margins. The rulers allow you to align, locate, and measure objects on the sheet. Disable the **Ruler** from the **Show** group on the **View** tab. 5️⃣

7. Adjust the contents of the sheet to the print area so that it can be printed in just one page. Click the **Page Layout** tab on the **Ribbon**.

8. In this case, you want to adjust the sheet to one page in height and one in width. Click the arrowhead button in the width field, in the **Scale to Fit** group, and select the **1 page** option. 6️⃣

9. Click the arrowhead button in the **Height** field and select the **1 page** option as well.

10. The **Status Bar** indicates that the workbook only has one page. To finish this exercise, click on the first icon in the view access group on the **Status Bar** to go back to the **Normal** view. 7️⃣

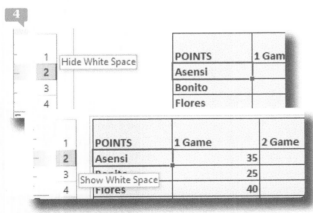

Click on the space that appears between the row and column headers and the spreadsheet to hide or unhide the space taken up by the margin.

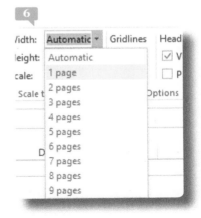

Select the width and height adjustments you need from the **Scale to Fit** group on the **Page Layout** tab.

You can show different elements of the sheet from the **Show** group.

Setting a print area

A PRINT AREA IS ONE OR MORE RANGES that have been selected for printing when you do not want to print the whole worksheet. When you set a printing area and then save the document, the area is saved as well. If you make a selection, print it, and do not save it as a print area, the program will not remember it.

1. To set a print area, select the cell range that you want to print. Use the **Shift + click** shortcut to create the range. 🔲

2. Click on the **Page Layout** tab and click on the **Print Area** command in the **Page Setup** group.

3. This command allows you to create and delete print areas. Click on the **Set Print Area** option. 🔲

4. A dotted line outlines the cell range and the **Print_Area** appears in the name box. 🔲 Once the print area has been set, you can go to the **Print** dialog box and indicate that you only want to print that area or you want, to skip that area. Click on the **File** tab and select the **Print** option. 🔲

1

	A	B	C	D	E
1	POINTS	1 Game	2 Game	3 Game	Total
2	Asensi	35	15	25	75
3	Bonito	25	25	25	75
4	Flores	40	30	10	80
5	Álvarez	10	25	50	85
6	Vera	60	10	25	95
7	Nerín	30	25	40	95
8	Balaguer	25	45	30	100
9	Pérez	25	55	45	125
10	Smith	30	25	55	110

Use the **Shift** key to select a cell range.

2

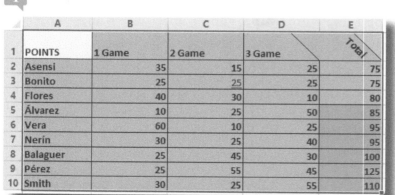

You will find all the necessary tools to set a print area in the **Page Setup** group on the **Page Layout** tab.

3

Notice that the print area stands out because it is outlined by a dotted line.

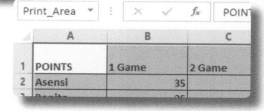

090

5. This will open the **Print** tab. In the **Settings** section **Print Active Sheets** is enabled by default. Remember that, when you set a print area, Excel interprets its contents as the selected page, which you can see in the Live Preview, on the right. Pull down this field's drop-down menu, select the **Ignore Print Area** option, and notice that there is no selected print area in the Live Preview. [5]

6. In order to only print the print area that you have set, disable the **Ignore Print Area** option again.

7. Go back to the sheet and, if it is not selected yet, select the **Page Layout** tab.

8. Notice that the **Ribbon** has a tools group called **Scale to Fit**, which allows you to modify the scale of the Print area. To finish the exercise, click on the **Print Area** command in the **Page Setup** group and click on **Clear Print Area**. [6]

9. If you want Excel to remember the information that corresponds to the print area you have set, save the workbook while keeping it selected.

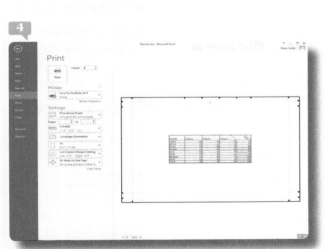

Go to the **Print** tab and notice that if you keep the **Print Active Sheets** option enabled when you set a print area, Excel will only print that area.

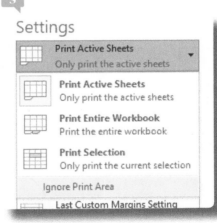

You can both create and delete a print area from the **Page Setup** group.

Turning text into columns

THE DATA TO COLUMNS COMMAND, in the Tools group on the Data tab, opens the Convert Text To Column Wizard, which allows you to split the contents of simple cells into several columns. This tool is particularly useful, for example, to separate first names and last names into different columns.

1. Enter a short list of first names and last names in a blank sheet from your workbook.

2. Select the cell range that includes the text you want to convert: Select the cell that contains the first name in the list, press and hold down the **Shift** key and click on the cell with the last name. 🔲

3. On the **Data** tab, click on the **Text to Columns** command in the **Data Tools** group. 🔲

4. The **Convert Text to Columns Wizard** opens with three steps to follow. For the first step you have to indicate whether the data you are going to convert is delimited or a fixed width. Select the **Delimited** option and click on the **Next** button. 🔲

5. In the second step you will define what type of separator you will use for the data. In the preview you can see how this will

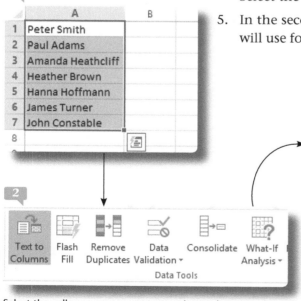

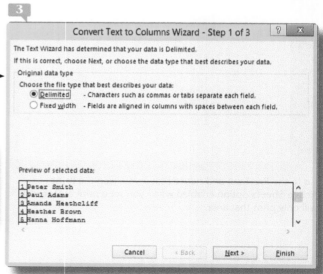

Select the cell range you want to turn into columns and click the **Text to Columns** too in order to access the **Convert Text to Columns Wizard**.

091

affect your data. In this case, the delimiter between the first name and the last name is a space. In the **Delimiters** section, disable the **Tab** option and enable the **Space** option.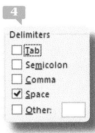

6. Check the result in the preview box. Now the first names and the last names are shown in two different columns. Click on the **Next** button.

7. In the third step, you will set a format for the contents of each column. Notice that the default format for all columns is **General**; you will change it to **Text**. Keep the first column selected in the preview and click on the **Text** option button.

8. Repeat this action with the second column.

9. You also have to specify in what part of the sheet the table will go. By default it will be placed in the first of the selected cells, so that the table will substitute for the text, but you can place it anywhere in order to keep the original text. If you need to, you can minimize the Wizard by clicking the icon that appears on the right of the **Destination** text box.

10. Click on a blank cell to select it and maximize the Wizard by clicking on the button that appears on the right of the text box.

11. Once you have set the conditions for the conversion, click on the **Finish** button and see the result.

In the second step of the Wizard, select the type of delimiter that is used between elements.

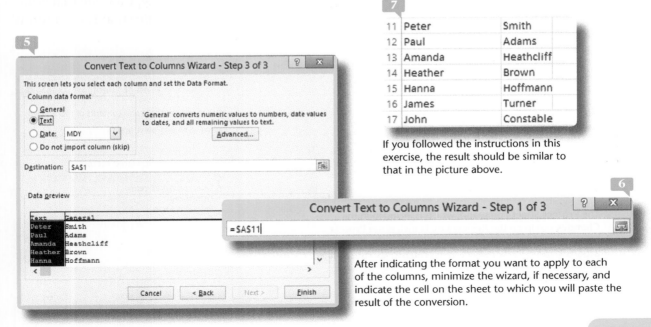

If you followed the instructions in this exercise, the result should be similar to that in the picture above.

After indicating the format you want to apply to each of the columns, minimize the wizard, if necessary, and indicate the cell on the sheet to which you will paste the result of the conversion.

Protecting the sheet

IMPORTANT

The **Protect Sheet** function can also be enabled from the contextual menu on each sheet label.

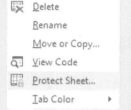

IN ORDER TO AVOID CHANGES to a spreadsheet, Excel comes with several built-in protection tools included in the Changes group on the Review tab. You can protect the selected sheet or the whole open workbook. This function protects formulas and cell values and allows you to modify the contents of previously defined certain ranges. It also allows you to restrict access to only those who have an appropriate password.

1. Imagine you want the data in your sheet to be read-only and not editable. For that, you will need to protect the sheet. Go to the **Review** tab on the **Ribbon** and click on the **Protect Sheet** command in the **Changes** group. 🗨

2. The **Protect Sheet** dialog box appears. Notice that in the **Allow all users of this worksheet to** box only the two options that allow you to select locked cells and to select unlocked cells are checked. With these settings you can protect all the objects contained in the sheet, but remember that you can use the **Allow Users to Edit Ranges** option to define an editable range within this sheet. Click on the **OK** button. 🗨

3. Select any cell with contents and try to type a value that is different from the current one. You will notice that Excel informs

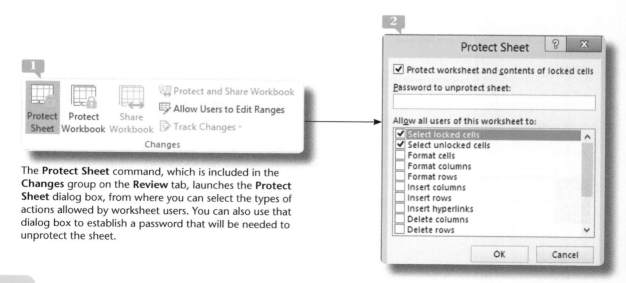

The **Protect Sheet** command, which is included in the **Changes** group on the **Review** tab, launches the **Protect Sheet** dialog box, from where you can select the types of actions allowed by worksheet users. You can also use that dialog box to establish a password that will be needed to unprotect the sheet.

you that the cells on this sheet are protected and therefore read-only. Click the **OK** button.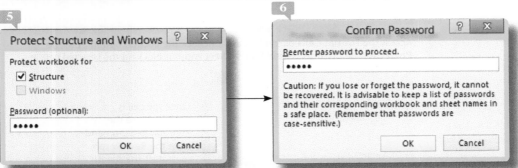

4. Click the **Unprotect Sheet** button to remove the protection.

5. The **Protect Workbook** command allows you to protect the structures and the windows of a workbook, making it impossible to change the number of sheets, change their order, hide them, resize the windows, etc. You can also prevent a workbook from being unprotected by using passwords. In this case, you will protect the structure of the workbook. Click on the **Protect Workbook** command.

6. The **Protect Structure and Windows** dialog box opens with the **Structure** option selected and the cursor in the **Password (optional)** field. Type your name in that box, for example, and click **OK**.

7. Type the password again in the **Reenter password to proceed** box and click **OK**.

8. To make sure that all the work options on the sheet are now disabled, right-click on the label of the selected cell.

9. It is indeed impossible to insert or to delete sheets, to rename them, etc. In order to unprotect the workbook, click the **Protect Workbook** command, type your password in the **Unprotect Workbook** box, and click on the **OK** button.

In order to protect the structure and the windows of a book, you need to go to the **Protect Workbook** command in the **Changes** group.

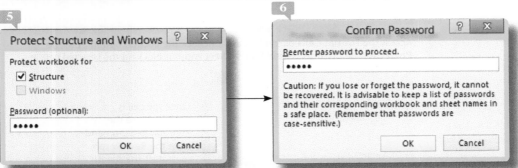

If you try to edit the contents of a protected cell, a warning message pops up informing you of the impossibility to carry out such action.

If you want to increase the amount of protection on the workbook structure, insert a password and confirm it.

Blocking and unblocking cells

A COMPLETELY BLOCKED SPREADSHEET is not very useful and only makes sense when it is a read-only document, as if it were printed matter. The correct protection for a table is to prevent others from editing formulas but allowing them to enter data in the variables.

1. Imagine you want to protect your worksheet in such a way that a particular cell may not be edited, –is not blocked. Select that cell and go to the **Home** tab on the **Ribbon**.

2. Click on the **Format** command in the **Cells** group, make sure that the **Lock cell** option is selected from the drop-down menu and click on the **Format Cells** option to access the **Format Cells** dialog box.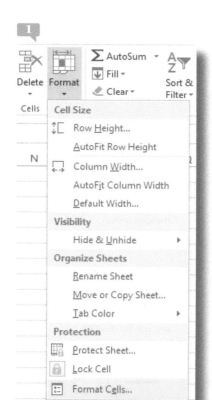

3. In the **Format Cells** dialog box, click on the **Protection** tab and make sure that the **Locked** option is selected here as well. Uncheck it and click on the **OK** button.

4. Next, go to the **Review** tab and click on the **Protect Sheet** command.

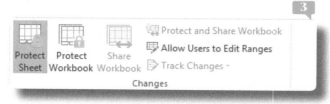

Access the **Format Cells** dialog box and uncheck the **Locked** option from the **Protection** tab in order to protect the sheet without blocking the selected cell.

Once the cell is unlocked, use the appropriate command from the **Review** tab to protect the sheet.

093

5. Keep the options as they appear in the **Protect Sheet** dialog box and click on the **OK** button.

6. All the cells in the sheet are locked, except the one you chose. Check by typing in the selected cell and clicking on the **Enter** icon.

7. The contents of an unblocked cell can be edited but not the format when the sheet is protected. To verify that, go to the **Home** tab again and click on the **Format** command in the **Cells** group.

8. All the options in this menu that have to do with cell editing are disabled. Click on the **Unprotect Sheet** option.

9. You will now enable the **Locked** option in the **Format** dialog box of the selected cell. This time, right-click on the selected cell and select the appropriate option from the contextual menu to access the **Format Cells** dialog box.

10. Go to the **Protection** tab, check the **Locked** check box and click on the **OK** button to finish the exercise.

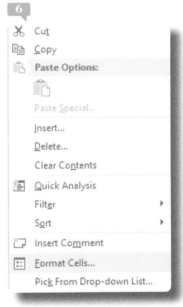

Remember that you can access the **Format Cells** dialog box from the **Format** command on the **Home** tab or from the Cells contextual menu.

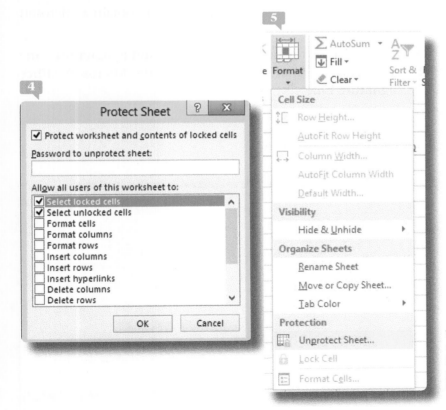

When you protect a sheet that contains a blocked cell, you can modify the contents of that cell but you cannot edit it. For that, you will have to unprotect the sheet.

Signing documents

MICROSOFT OFFICE DIGITAL SIGNATURES combine the familiarity of signatures on paper and the advantages of digital ones. In this exercise, you will learn how to add a signature at the end of the document. This signature line specifies the person who has to sign the document. A signature line will be inserted with the signatory's personal data where the person will have to sign either manually once the document has been printed or digitally.

1. For this exercise, you will keep using the **Points3** sample file. Click on the **Insert** tab.

2. Click on the arrowhead button on the **Add a Signature Line** command, which is in the **Text** group just below the **WordArt** command.

3. Select the **Add Signature Services** option.

4. A page will open in your default browser where you will find all the necessary information necessary to obtain a Microsoft Office digital certificate. Close this page.

5. Click on the arrowhead button of the **Add a Signature Line** command again and this time, select the **Microsoft Office Signature Line**.

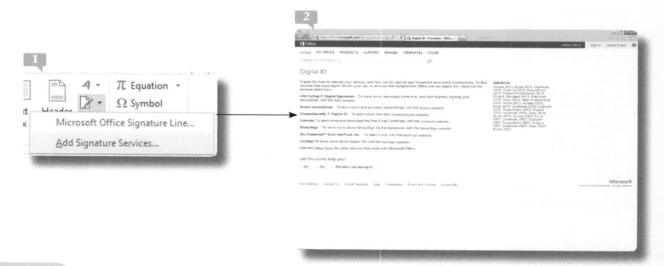

6. This launches the **Signature Setup** dialog box in which you have to add all the information about the signer so that it is visible in the signature line. Since you will be the one to sign the document, start by entering your name in the **Suggested signer** text box.

7. Fill out the **Suggested signer's title** and the **Suggested signer's e-mail address** text boxes.

8. Check the **Allow the signer to add comments** in the **Sign dialog** check box so that you can add some comments later on. Make sure the **Show sign date in signature line** option is checked and click on the **OK** button. 🗨3

9. The signature line is then inserted in the Excel worksheet in the form of an image that you can resize and move. Right-click on the signature line and select the **Format Picture** option from the contextual menu. 🗨4

10. Select the **Size** tab in the **Format Picture** dialog box.

11. In the **Height** field type **4**, in the **Width** field type 8, and click the **OK** button. 🗨5

12. Click and hold down the mouse on the signature line you have inserted and move it to a spot that is convenient for you.

13. To finish this exercise, deselect the signature line and use the **Ctrl + S** shortcut to save the changes.

The size and location of the signature line can be modified from the **Format Picture** dialog box. 5

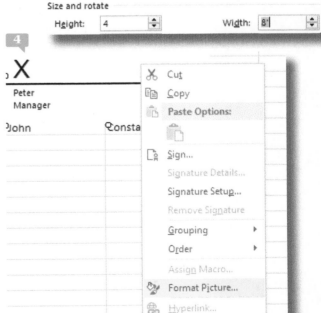

You have to add all the information you want listed on the signature line in the **Signature Setup** dialog box.

Recovering documents

IMPORTANT

If Excel closes suddenly due to an error or a power outage, on start up the **Document Recovery** task pane will appear by default on the left side of the Excel interface. This pane can show up to three versions of the document you were working on before the error or the power outage occurred.

THE EXCEL DOCUMENT RECOVERY SECURITY FEATURE recovers the documents you are working on in case the computer becomes irresponsive or shows an unexpected error that forces you to restart it or turn it off.

1. In this exercise you will learn about the document AutoRecover options in Excel 2013. Click on the **Options** button on the **File** tab to access the **Excel Options** dialog box.

2. Click the **Save** option in the categories panel on the left.

3. On this tab you can specify how long the program should keep the AutoRecover information and determine in what path it will be saved. Keep the default AutoRecover options and click on the **OK** button.

4. Imagine that there has been a power shortage or that there has been some kind of error in the program just after you made a change without saving it. To create this situation, you will force a shutdown of your computer by using the **Ctrl +Alt + Del** shortcut.

5. Some basic Windows options will appear on your screen. Select the one named **Task Manager**.

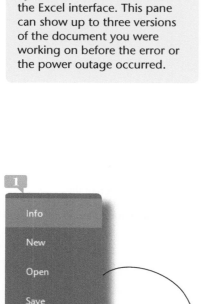

Customize how workbooks are saved.

Save workbooks

Save files in this format: Excel Workbook (*.xlsx)

☑ Save AutoRecover information every 10 ⬍ minutes

   ☑ Keep the last autosaved version if I close without saving

AutoRecover file location: C:\Users\Nuria\AppData\Roamin

☐ Don't show the Backstage when opening or saving files

☑ Show additional places for saving, even if sign-in may be required.

☐ Save to Computer by default

Default local file location: C:\Users\Nuria\Documents

In Excel, the **File AutoSave** options can be found on the **Save** tab in the **Excel Options** dialog box. From there, you can set up the place where you want AutoRecover files to be stored or disable this feature for a specific document, etc.

095

6. The **Task Manager** dialog box, which has been noticeably improved in Windows 8, the version you are using in this manual, will open. On the **Processes** tab, you will see all the programs that are open at the moment. Click on **Microsoft Excel** and click the **End Task** button.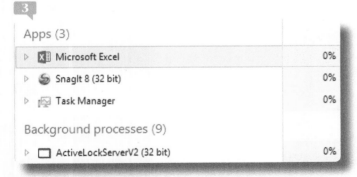

7. Click on the **X** on its **Title Bar** to close the **Task Manager**.

8. Excel has closed. You will now open the program again from the new Windows Home screen. Click on the **Windows** key to access that screen, locate the Excel 2013 thumbnail, and click on it.

9. When you open the program again, the **Recent Documents** panel will appear with the **Recovered** section added to it that indicates Excel has recovered a file that you might want to keep. Click on **Show Recovered Files**.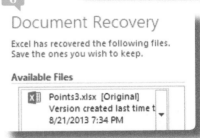

10. On the left of the work area the **Document Recovery** task pane will appear, which shows the last available version of your workbook. Click on it to recover it.

11. The selected document will open automatically and show up in the **Document Recovery** task pane, highlighted in black. 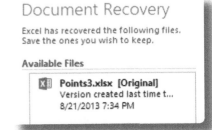 To finish this exercise, click on the Close button to close the **Document Recovery** panel.

Recovered

Excel has recovered files that you might want to keep.

Show Recovered Files

Recent

Points3.xlsx
My Documents » Excel 2013 Necessary Files

PowerPivot.xlsx
My Documents

PowerPivot2.xlsx
My Documents

Apps (3)

▷	Microsoft Excel	0%
▷	SnagIt 8 (32 bit)	0%
▷	Task Manager	0%

Background processes (9)

▷	ActiveLockServerV2 (32 bit)	0%

Document Recovery

Excel has recovered the following files. Save the ones you wish to keep.

Available Files

Points3.xlsx [Original]
Version created last time t
8/21/2013 7:34 PM

Access 2013

Excel 2013

The down arrow button on the available versions of recovered files includes the **Open, Save as, Delete,** and **Show Repairs** options.

Document Recovery

Excel has recovered the following files. Save the ones you wish to keep.

Available Files

Points3.xlsx [Original]
Version created last time t...
8/21/2013 7:34 PM

Inserting comments

IMPORTANT

You can define how you want cells with comments to be displayed on your sheet in the **Display** section of the **Advanced** tab of the **Excel Options** window. By default, the option in which only comment indicators are displayed and comments appear when they are activated is enabled.

For cells with comments, show:

- ○ No comments or indicators
- ○ Indicators only, and comments
- ● Comments and indicators

INSERTING A COMMENT IN A CELL does not take up any space and it can be very useful as a reminder or hint. The only indication that a cell contains a comment is a discreet red triangle in its upper right corner.

1. Select the cell **A1** (Points) in the **Points3** workbook, activate the **Review** tab in the **Ribbon**, and click on the **New Comment** command. 🔲¹

2. A yellow box with the username corresponding to your computer and a blinking cursor, which indicates where you can start typing your message, appears. Type some sample text 🔲² and select the cell again to finish entering the comment.

3. If you've just realized that you didn't type in the text correctly and you wish to correct it, click on the **Show All Comments** command in the **Comments** group. 🔲³

4. Excel displays the yellow comment box again. Click on it, modify the text, and click on the selected cell to finish your modification.

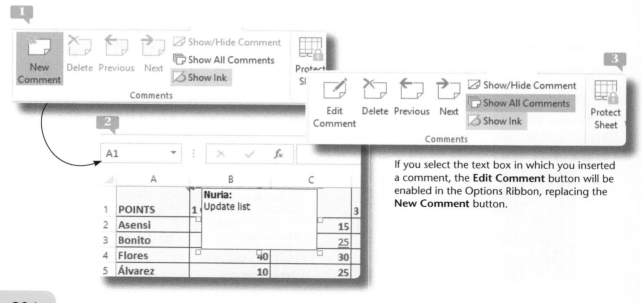

If you select the text box in which you inserted a comment, the **Edit Comment** button will be enabled in the Options Ribbon, replacing the **New Comment** button.

096

5. Hide the comment by disabling the **Show All Comments** option.

6. Select another cell in your sheet, right-click on it to open its pop-up menu and choose the **Insert comment** option.

7. Type some sample text in the **Comment** tag and click on the cell to confirm it.

8. Up to this point, you have seen how to insert and modify comments. Generally, comments can only be read by hovering the mouse over the cell in which they are inserted, or by clicking on the **Show/Hide Comment** command when the cell is selected. Click on the **Show/Hide Comment** command.

9. And to show all comments, click on the **Show All Comments** button again.

10. The **Previous** and **Next** buttons allow you to navigate through the comments, and the **Delete** command allows you to delete them from the sheet. Keep in mind that this command is only active when a cell that contains a comment is selected. Click on it to delete your last comment.

11. Select the other cell in which you inserted a comment, which now displays a small right triangle in its upper right corner, and click on the **Delete** command again.

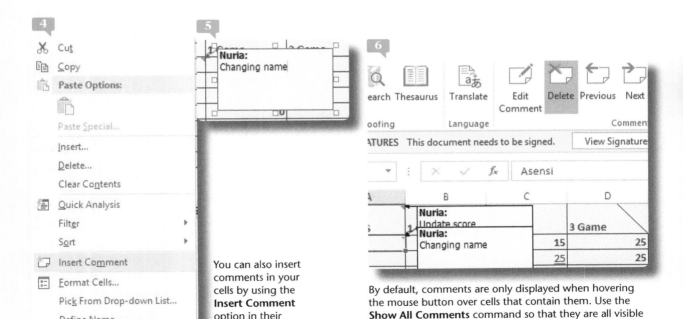

You can also insert comments in your cells by using the **Insert Comment** option in their pop-up menus.

By default, comments are only displayed when hovering the mouse button over cells that contain them. Use the **Show All Comments** command so that they are all visible on the sheet.

Sending by e-mail

IMPORTANT

You can send of your workbook as a PDF file or as an XPS file by using those options in the **Share** command in the **File** tab.

THE E-MAIL OPTION IS LOCATED in the Share command in the File tab. This option adds the spreadsheet that is currently active as an attached file in an e-mail. Your currently configured e-mail client is used by default. When you give the order to send the message, it will be saved in the program's outbox.

1. Click on the **File** tab and click on the **Share** command.

2. Remember that, as a new feature in Excel 2013, it is now possible to share a book on the cloud, specifically in a SkyDrive storage space. Select the **Email** option.

3. This command includes all the options that allow you to send a copy of the book to other people, either as an e-mail message, in different formats, or using an Internet fax service. Click on the **Send as Attachment** option.

4. This opens the e-mail message window with the workbook attached, and its name as the subject. You can change the subject if you wish. Enter the recipient's name. Enter an e-mail address in the **To** field.

If you have the address to which you wish to send this message saved in your contacts, click on the **To** button to open your address book.

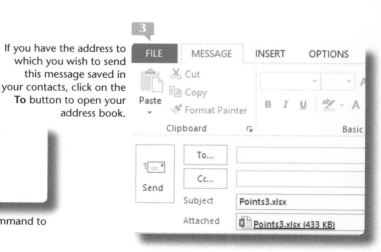

Use the **Send as Attachment** option in the **Share** command to send a workbook via e-mail.

097

5. If you wish, you can type some message text. Click on the text area in the message and insert some text that will accompany the attached file.

6. To send the message to the outbox in Outlook (or your usual e-mail client program), simply click on the **Send** button in the message header.

7. Now you will see if the message was correctly sent to the outbox in Outlook (or your default client), ready to be sent. Open your usual e-mail client.

8. This opens the program window, displaying the contents of the inbox. Click on the **Outbox** folder.

9. The message you created from Excel is displayed there. The paperclip next to the recipient's name indicates that it contains attached files, in this case, the book. In order to definitively send your message to the recipient, click on the **Send/ Receive All Folders** button.

10. Once the message is sent, close Outlook by clicking on the X in its **Title Bar**.

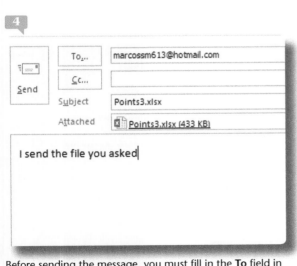

Before sending the message, you must fill in the **To** field in the header and, optionally, the Subject, CC, and message text fields.

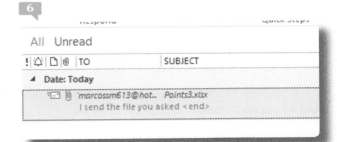

Click on the **Send** button to send the message to its recipient.

Inspecting a document

IMPORTANT

It is better to use the **Document Inspector** on a copy of the original document, as you cannot always restore the data deleted by the Inspector. For instance, if you delete rows, delete columns, or hide sheets that contain data, this can affect the calculations in your workbook. If you do not know the contents of these hidden elements, reveal them and review their contents before deleting them.

THE INSPECT DOCUMENT FUNCTION allows you to review a workbook to see if there is any private information, comments, hidden rows or columns, etc., and to delete them if necessary. This tool is especially practical when the workbook contains confidential information you do not wish to share with other users.

1. Continue working on the **Points3** file. If you want to share the document with other users and you want to delete any confidential information, comments, notes, etc., click on the **File** tab and click on the **Check for Issues** in the **Information** category.

2. This command includes the necessary tools to prepare the document to be distributed. In the emerging sub-menu, click on the **Inspect Document** option.

3. This opens the **Document Inspector**, in which you must select the hidden or private content you do not wish to include in the workbook you are about to share. With this tool you can find comments, annotations, document properties and personal information, invisible contents, etc. If you only

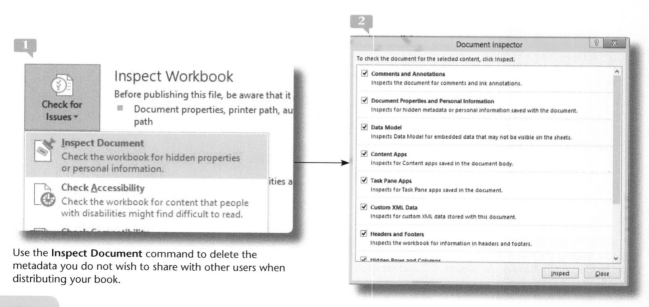

Use the **Inspect Document** command to delete the metadata you do not wish to share with other users when distributing your book.

098

wish to find and delete the comments and annotations and the document properties, disable the remaining options by clicking on their check boxes.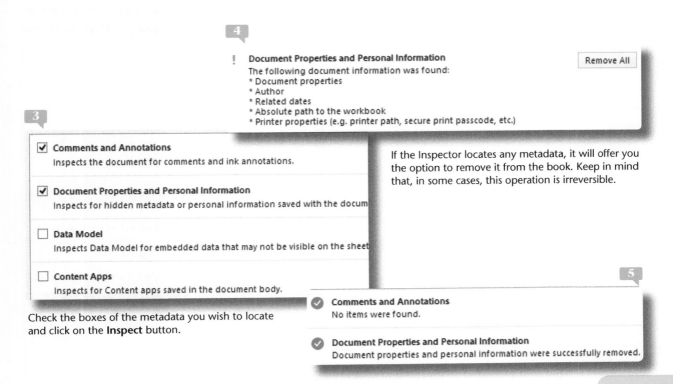

4. Once you have determined which elements you wish to find in the workbook, click on the **Inspect** button.

5. The **Document Inspector** locates the information you specified and offers to remove it before distributing the book to other users. Click on the **Remove All** button if your document includes comments, annotations, or properties.

6. The Inspector now informs you that the data was removed correctly. Once the revision is over, you can inspect the book again (you can repeat this operation as many times as is necessary) or close the Inspector. Click on the **Reinspect** button.

7. Check the options you wish to inspect and click on the **Inspect** button.

8. Click on the **Close** button in the **Document Inspector** window.

If you have deleted the properties of the book, you can open the **Document Properties**, also via the **Information** command, to check if they no longer appear.

4

> **! Document Properties and Personal Information**   [Remove All]
> The following document information was found:
> * Document properties
> * Author
> * Related dates
> * Absolute path to the workbook
> * Printer properties (e.g. printer path, secure print passcode, etc.)

3

> ☑ **Comments and Annotations**
> Inspects the document for comments and ink annotations.
>
> ☑ **Document Properties and Personal Information**
> Inspects for hidden metadata or personal information saved with the docum
>
> ☐ **Data Model**
> Inspects Data Model for embedded data that may not be visible on the sheet
>
> ☐ **Content Apps**
> Inspects for Content apps saved in the document body.

If the Inspector locates any metadata, it will offer you the option to remove it from the book. Keep in mind that, in some cases, this operation is irreversible.

Check the boxes of the metadata you wish to locate and click on the **Inspect** button.

5

> ✓ **Comments and Annotations**
> No items were found.
>
> ✓ **Document Properties and Personal Information**
> Document properties and personal information were successfully removed.

Mark as final

TO MAKE A BOOK READ-ONLY, THUS PREVENTING it from being modified by accident by unauthorized users, you can use the Mark as Final function. When a book is marked as final, an icon appears indicating it in the Status Bar, and the editing, writing, and reviewing tools are disabled and the status property is changed to Final.

1. In this exercise you will mark the book you are working with as final and, after seeing how this function works, we will return it to its original state. Click on the **File** tab and click on the **Protect Workbook** command in the **Info** category to see which options it includes.

2. Click on the **Mark as Final** option.

3. A warning window appears, telling you that you must mark the book as final before saving it. Click on the **OK** button in this window.

4. In the informational window, when you mark a workbook as final, its **Status** property is changed to **Final**, so that users you

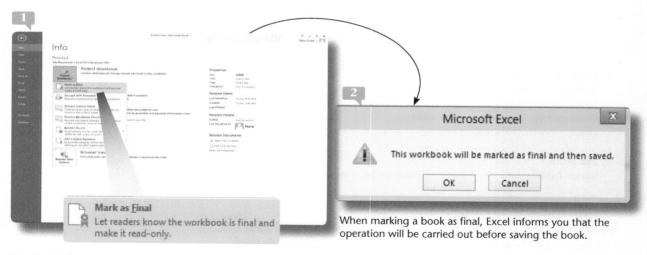

When marking a book as final, Excel informs you that the operation will be carried out before saving the book.

Use the **Mark as Final** option in the **Protect Workbook** command of the **File** tab to mark a book as final so that it cannot be modified by other users.

099

share it with will know that it is the final version of that workbook. Likewise, editing and design commands are disabled so the workbook cannot be modified. Click on the **OK** button in this dialog box.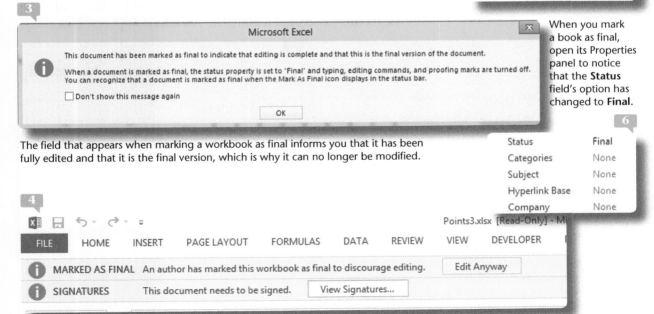

5. An informational bar appears over the work area telling you that the book has been marked as final, and it offers the possibility to edit it anyway. Likewise, an icon that looks like a cap has appeared in the book's **Status Bar**. Click on the **Home** tab and notice that the commands in the **Ribbon** are now disabled.

6. Check to see if the workbook's status is **Final**. Click on the **File** tab and click on the **Info** option.

7. The **Protect Workbook** function also tells you that the workbook has been marked as final. Select the **Show All Properties** option in the **Properties** command.

8. This makes all document properties visible, and you can see that the field does, indeed, display the **Final** option to indicate that it is finished.

9. To edit a workbook that has been marked as final, simply disable this option. Click on the **Protect Workbook** command and deselect the **Mark as Final** option.

IMPORTANT

Notice that, when a workbook is marked as final, the **Save** option in the **File** tab is disabled, as a book marked as final cannot be modified.

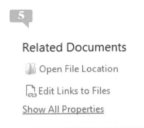

Related Documents

Open File Location

Edit Links to Files

Show All Properties

When you mark a book as final, open its Properties panel to notice that the **Status** field's option has changed to **Final**.

Status	Final
Categories	None
Subject	None
Hyperlink Base	None
Company	None

Microsoft Excel

This document has been marked as final to indicate that editing is complete and that this is the final version of the document.

When a document is marked as final, the status property is set to "Final" and typing, editing commands, and proofing marks are turned off. You can recognize that a document is marked as final when the Mark As Final icon displays in the status bar.

☐ Don't show this message again

OK

The field that appears when marking a workbook as final informs you that it has been fully edited and that it is the final version, which is why it can no longer be modified.

Points3.xlsx [Read-Only] - Mi

FILE   HOME   INSERT   PAGE LAYOUT   FORMULAS   DATA   REVIEW   VIEW   DEVELOPER

ⓘ MARKED AS FINAL   An author has marked this workbook as final to discourage editing.   Edit Anyway

ⓘ SIGNATURES   This document needs to be signed.   View Signatures...

Changing browser view options

IMPORTANT

Keep in mind that, when you publish a workbook on the web, even though you limit the items that users can view in the browser, the complete workbook will still be available in Excel.

ONE OF THE MOST INTERESTING new features included in the Office 2013 suite is the ability to share documents created with its different applications on a virtual space, on the cloud (for instance, on SkyDrive, as you saw in a previous exercise). In the Information category of the File menu you can find the option that allows you to choose what users will be able to see when an Excel workbook is displayed online.

1. Click on the **File** tab, activate the **Info** category, and click on the **Browser View Options**. 🗩

2. This opens the **Browser View Options** window. In the **Show** and **Parameters** tabs you can select the sheets and items that will be displayed when the book is published online, as well as adding settings to specify which cells can be modified by the users. The **Entire Workbook** option in the **Show** tab is enabled by default, which means that all the sheets in the workbook will be displayed. Click on the arrow button in the **Entire Workbook** option and choose **Items in the Workbook**. 🗩

3. This reveals a list of items you have added to the workbook throughout these exercises (graphs, dynamic tables and ranges, in this example). Enable the **All Charts** option. 🗩

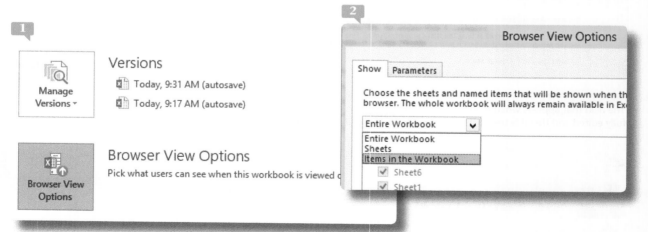

In Excel 2013 it's possible to publish a workbook in a **SharePoint** library, for instance, so that other users can edit it in a web browser without having the program installed on their computers.

100

4. Enable **PivotTable1**, click on the lower part of the **Vertical scroll bar** and enable the **All Named Ranges** option. 4

5. Go to the **Parameters** tab by clicking on it.

6. You can add settings to this tab to indicate which cells in the workbook can be modified in the browser. 5 Keep in mind that, in order to establish settings, you must previously assign names to individual cells that contain values in the different sheets. These cells are the ones you can use as parameters. If you have added parameters, you can delete them one by one or all at the same time by using the **Delete** and **Delete All** buttons. Click on the **OK** button in the **Browser View Options**.

7. In this example, a dialog box warns you that you have selected several elements with the same name, among which only one is available. Confirm that you wish to continue by clicking on the **Yes** button in this dialog box. 6

8. You have now configured your workbook to be published on the web. You can access the Browser View Options window to modify the options at any time. Finish the exercise by closing the Excel workbook.

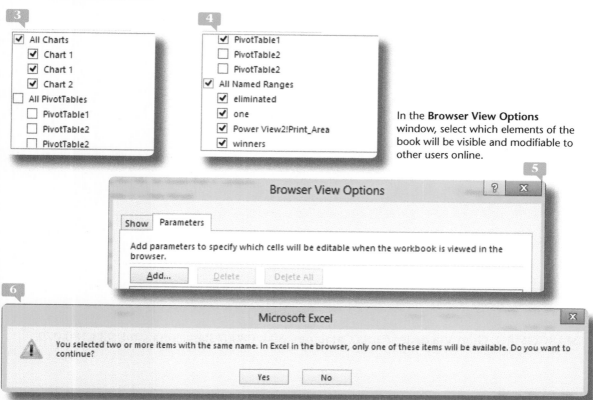

In the **Browser View Options** window, select which elements of the book will be visible and modifiable to other users online.

To continue learning ...

IF THIS BOOK HAS MET YOUR EXPECTATIONS

This book is part of a collection that covers the most commonly used and known software in all professional areas.

All books in the series have the same approach as the one that you have just finished. So, if you would like to know more about the new features of Office 2013 or other software packages, on the next page you will find other books in this collection.

MARCOMBO, Gran Via de les Corts Catalanes, 594, 08007 Barcelona - Tel. 933 180 079

PHOTO EDITING

If you want to know all the secrets of the most widely used and popular program for editing images, Learning Photoshop CS6 with 100 Practical Exercises is undoubtedly the book you are looking for.

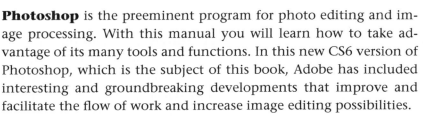

Photoshop is the preeminent program for photo editing and image processing. With this manual you will learn how to take advantage of its many tools and functions. In this new CS6 version of Photoshop, which is the subject of this book, Adobe has included interesting and groundbreaking developments that improve and facilitate the flow of work and increase image editing possibilities.

Using this book:

- You will get to know the new Crop in Perspective Tool.
- You will retouch images with incredible features such as Fill According to Content and the new Content-Aware Patch Tool.
- You will freely transform certain parts of an image.
- You will work on a new and spectacular 3D interface to achieve the best 3D effects.

COMPUTER-AIDED DESIGN

If you want to know all the secrets of design in one of the most valued programs out right now, Learning Illustrator CS6 with 100 Practical Exercises is undoubtedly the book you are looking for.

Illustrator the vector drawing application from Adobe, is an excellent tool for computer-aided design. Thanks to its amazing and powerful features, you can create original artwork using drawings and images. Use the 100 exercises in this book to expand your knowledge and discover the thousand and one possibilities hidden in this great program.

Using this book:

- Learn about the enhanced tools for creating patterns.
- Discover the improved image tracing tool that now provides clean lines and a perfect fit.
- Apply gradients on strokes to get interesting and striking results.

OPERATING SYSTEMS

If you want to know all the secrets of the most widely used operating system, Learning Windows 8 with 100 Practical Exercises is undoubtedly the book you are looking for.

Windows 8 is Microsoft's new version of its operating system loaded with many new functions. You'll see the changes that Microsoft has made as soon as you start your session: A new customizable start screen that displays icons that can access the programs and applications installed on your computer. The new Metro interface of Windows 8 is specially designed to work with touch-screen devices.

Using this book:

- Get to know the Metro interface of Windows 8.
- Practice with the Ribbon in Windows Explorer.
- Work with the new and advanced Task Manager.
- Learn how to use new security and maintenance tools to always keep your PC as safe as possible.

IMAGE RETOUCH

If you want to improve the appearance of your digital photos and create amazing compositions, Learning Image Retouch with Photoshop CS6 with 100 Practical Exercises is undoubtedly the book you are looking for.

Photoshop is the preeminent program for retouching photographs and image processing. With the help of this manual you will learn how to use the different tools, filters, and functions in order to improve the appearance of your digital photos and create amazing compositions.

Using this book:

- Learn how to correct typical defects in photographs taken by inexperienced photographers (overexposure, underexposure, blurs, keystoning, etc.).
- Discover simple but extraordinary techniques to retouch small defects in portraits of people (dark circles, flaws, wrinkles, etc.).